CAMPAIGN • 211

ACTIUM 31 BC

Downfall of Antony and Cleopatra

SI SHEPPARD ILLUSTRATED BY CHRISTA HOOK

Series editors Marcus Cowper and Nikolai Bogdanovic

First published in 2009 by Osprey Publishing
Midland House, West Way, Botley, Oxford OX2 0PH, UK
443 Park Avenue South, New York, NY 10016, USA
E-mail: info@ospreypublishing.com

ISBN 978 184603 405 3

PDF e-book ISBN: 978 1 84603 899 0

Editorial by Ilios Publishing, Oxford, UK (www.iliospublishing.com)
Design: The Black Spot
Index by Glyn Sutcliffe
Cartography: Map Studio, Romsey, Hants
Bird's-eye view artworks: The Black Spot
Typeset in Sabon and Myriad Pro
Originated by PPS Grasmere: Leeds
Printed in China through Worldprint Ltd.

09 10 11 12 13   10 9 8 7 6 5 4 3 2 1

A CIP catalogue record for this book is available from the British Library.

FOR A CATALOGUE OF ALL BOOKS PUBLISHED BY OSPREY MILITARY AND
AVIATION PLEASE CONTACT:

NORTH AMERICA
Osprey Direct, c/o Random House Distribution Center, 400 Hahn Road,
Westminster, MD 21157
E-mail: uscustomerservice@ospreypublishing.com

ALL OTHER REGIONS
Osprey Direct
The Book Service Ltd, Distribution Centre, Colchester Road, Frating Green,
Colchester, Essex, CO7 7DW
E-mail: customerservice@ospreypublishing.com

www.ospreypublishing.com

DEDICATION

To my shining star, Laurissa.

IMAGE CREDITS

Unless otherwise stated, the photographic images that appear in this work
are from the author's collection.

ARTIST'S NOTE

Readers may care to note that the original paintings from which the colour
plates in this book were prepared are available for private sale. The
Publishers retain all reproduction copyright whatsoever. All enquiries
should be addressed to:

Scorpio Gallery,
PO Box 475,
Hailsham,
East Sussex
BN27 2SL,
UK

The Publishers regret that they can enter into no correspondence upon
this matter.

THE WOODLAND TRUST

Osprey Publishing are supporting the Woodland Trust, the UK's leading
woodland conservation charity, by funding the dedication of trees.

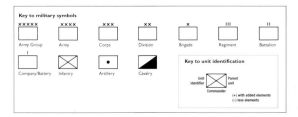

CONTENTS

The Roman world from the Pact of Brundisium (40 BC) to the fall of Ptolemaic Egypt (30 BC)

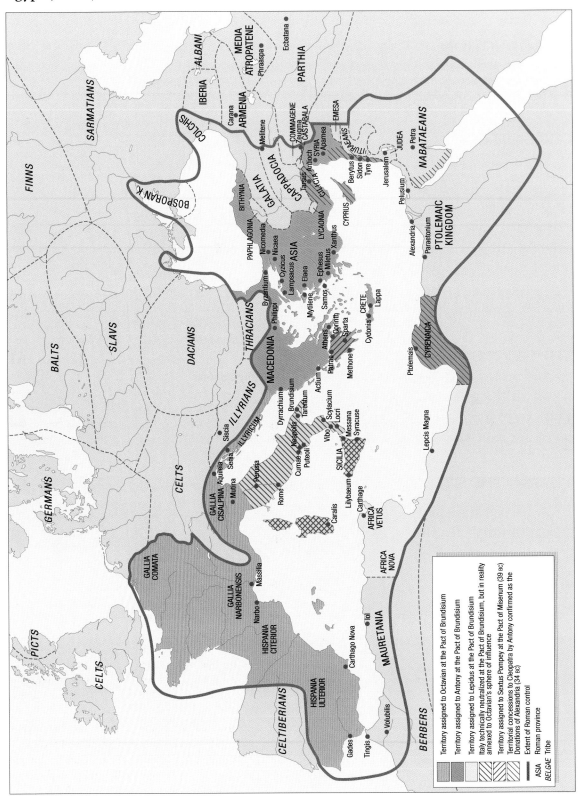

Legend:

- Territory assigned to Octavian at the Pact of Brundisium
- Territory assigned to Antony at the Pact of Brundisium
- Territory assigned to Lepidus at the Pact of Brundisium
- Italy technically neutralized at the Pact of Brundisium, but in reality annexed to Octavian's sphere of influence
- Territory assigned to Sextus Pompey at the Pact of Misenum (39 BC)
- Territorial concessions to Cleopatra by Antony confirmed as the Donations of Alexandria (34 BC)
- Extent of Roman control
- ASIA   Roman province
- *BELGAE*   Tribe

INTRODUCTION

THE SITUATION IN THE WEST

The Pact of Brundisium (Brindisi) in 40 BC, by which the triumvirs Antony and Octavian stepped back from the brink of total war and agreed to divide the Roman world between them, was seized upon with a desperate, almost manic zeal by the populace at large. Senators and citizens alike embraced the settlement as a viable conflict resolution mechanism that could balance the chronic structural flaws of the Roman socio-political system and bring an end to decades of endemic civil war. Even more remarkable than the fact that peace was only secured via an extra-constitutional arrangement between rival warlords arrived at behind closed doors was the fact that, by this time, informal understandings such as these were in reality the only force capable of preventing the Roman social fabric from unravelling altogether. The Republic, which had endured against all foes, foreign and domestic, for over four and a half centuries, was in its terminal phase. Having long ago lost its monopoly of violence, it had become hollow to the point where the only authority it retained was purely symbolic.

Much was made of Antony's marriage to Octavia, the sister of Octavian, to seal the rapprochement between the two men. Among those caught up in the enthusiasm was the poet Virgil, whose *IV Eclogue* celebrated 'the end of the men of Iron' and anticipated the birth of a child heralding the dawn of an age of gold:

> The boy will mingle with the gods and the great heroes who
> Consort with them, and they shall see him rule the world,
> The son of those whose deeds have granted peace on earth

This prodigal son in fact turned out to be a girl, Antonia, born the following year. But even if the child had been a boy, uniting both bloodlines in a common heir, the settlement at Brundisium would only have provided a temporary reprieve from the struggle to define what – or who – would succeed the dying Republic.

The respective claims of Antony and Octavian to the legacy of Caesar made a winner-takes-all clash between them ultimately inevitable. But, despite the smouldering mutual hostility that charged their every encounter with an underlying tension, this final confrontation was repeatedly postponed as each struggled to secure his position within the power vacuum of the terminal

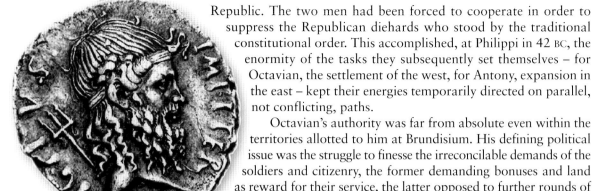

A coin of Sextus Pompey, featuring a portrait of his patron Neptune, the god of the sea, on the obverse. According to Suetonius, after losing his fleet in a storm during the abortive invasion of Sicily in 38 BC, Octavian vowed he would conquer 'in spite of Neptune', and at the next Circensian Games would not allow the statue of that god to take its accustomed place in the procession. (Classical Numismatic Group)

Republic. The two men had been forced to cooperate in order to suppress the Republican diehards who stood by the traditional constitutional order. This accomplished, at Philippi in 42 BC, the enormity of the tasks they subsequently set themselves – for Octavian, the settlement of the west, for Antony, expansion in the east – kept their energies temporarily directed on parallel, not conflicting, paths.

Octavian's authority was far from absolute even within the territories allotted to him at Brundisium. His defining political issue was the struggle to finesse the irreconcilable demands of the soldiers and citizenry, the former demanding bonuses and land as reward for their service, the latter opposed to further rounds of the taxation and confiscation required to provide them. A single misstep could provoke either side to shift decisively into the camp of one of two potential rivals at large within his defined sphere of influence. Technically, Octavian was required to extend to Marcus Lepidus the courtesies due to the third member of the Triumvirate. But Lepidus had been effectively marginalized by his erstwhile colleagues. Relegated to governing Africa, he commanded little respect even there.

Far more serious was the threat posed by Sextus Pompey, the outlaw whose naval power had enabled him to not only maintain Sicily as a haven for all those opposed to the new order (from fugitive slaves to proscribed senators), but also to impose himself upon the Triumvirate as a fourth player in the terminal Republican era. In exchange for relaxing his stranglehold over the commercial shipping vital to the survival of Rome, at the Pact of Misenum in 39 BC Sextus had been confirmed in his possession of Sicily, Sardinia and Corsica and granted custody of the Peloponnese.

The existence of this little nautical empire strung out along his lines of communication and supply was nettlesome to Octavian, but the real danger lay in blood not water. Rome placed great stock in inheritance, and Sextus, as the sole surviving heir to Pompey the Great, could draw upon the respect accorded the one name that still resonated in the popular imagination in the same league as Caesar. A showdown between the two scions of their respective patrimonies could not be avoided. As Dio observes, 'They were bound, of course, to go to war in any case, even if they had found no excuse.' But justifications for the resumption of hostilities were in fact not hard to find. Octavian sent a clear message in late 39 BC when he ended his arranged marriage to Scribonia, the sister of Sextus' father-in-law ('utterly disgusted', he wrote afterwards, 'with her disagreeable temper') on the very day she bore him a daughter, Julia. He subsequently induced Tiberius Nero to divorce his wife Livia, then pregnant with their second child, so he could marry her three days after she gave birth.

THE FIRST CLASH BETWEEN OCTAVIAN AND SEXTUS

None of the signatories at Misenum acted in good faith. Sextus accused Antony of stripping the Peloponnese of its assets prior to transferring his authority. Octavian accused Sextus of harbouring deserters contrary to the treaty, expanding the naval forces under his command, and maintaining his garrisons on the mainland. Sextus responded by unleashing his privateers against the ports and coastal shipping of Italy, effectively severing the critical grain imports upon which Rome depended. Their exaggerated expectations of a swift return to peace and prosperity dissolving into inflation and hunger, the people groaned that the triumvirs had only succeeded in adding a fourth partner to their tyranny.

Octavian was both held responsible for the crisis and obligated to resolve it. A military response was problematic, complicated by two factors. First, Octavian lacked the financial reserves necessary to undertake offensive action, and imposing taxes to fund the war effort would only further contribute to disaffection from his regime. As Shakespeare's Sextus succinctly noted in *Antony and Cleopatra*, 'Caesar gets money where he loses hearts.' Second, Sextus ruled the waves. The clique of freedmen in his inner circle were skilled and experienced naval commanders, and they and their crews were superior to anything Octavian had at his disposal. They had already proved their mettle; Octavian had mobilized for the invasion of Sicily in late 42 BC, but, his admiral Salvidienus Rufus having been outmatched in an encounter off the Scyllaean promontory, could not secure control of the straits, the necessary prerequisite to an amphibious operation, and had been constrained to withdraw.

Sextus, conversely, was vulnerable on two fronts. First, the only strategic option available to him was an essentially reactive one. This passivity baffled the ancient writers; Appian commented that Sextus must have been 'stricken with some strange aberration, [for] he never pursued an aggressive policy against his foes, although fortune offered him many opportunities; he only defended himself.' But the fact was Sextus, by himself, simply lacked the resources to take the fight to Octavian. His only hope was to hold Octavian at bay long enough for exasperation in Rome to boil over into the streets; in the aftermath, Pompey's heir would sail in to pick up the pieces. However, Sextus could properly be chastised for his failure to seek, let alone secure, an accommodation with a more powerful ally. His bridgehead to the west would have been of inestimable value to Brutus and Cassius prior to Philippi and Antony afterwards. But by choice, Sextus would stand, or fall, a lone wolf.

Second, Sextus never succeeded in constructing any kind of distinctive collective identity within the territories under his control that could have endowed his regime with institutional legitimacy. The sole force binding together a disparate community of renegades was a cult of personality centred on Sextus himself.

This lack of institutional loyalty worked in Octavian's favour when Sextus fell out with the most powerful of his freedmen, Menas, the governor of his outlying islands. Summoned by Sextus to account for the defalcation of grain and gold under his charge, Menas seized and executed the delegation sent to demand his impeachment. Having immediately sought terms from Octavian, he surrendered control of Sardinia, Corsica, three legions of soldiers, a considerable body of light-armed troops, and an unknown, but probably substantial, number of ships.

Having thus reduced Sextus to little more than his redoubt of Sicily, Octavian mobilized for a pre-emptive strike that would eliminate his rival altogether. Seeking a united front, Octavian dispatched urgent messages summoning his triumviral colleagues Lepidus and Antony to a conference at Brundisium. Lepidus ignored the appeal; Antony duly arrived, but when Octavian failed to appear by the specified date he returned to Athens. Antony had nothing to gain by the eradication of Sextus, but he had no way of preventing it; to register his disapproval he wrote to Octavian urging him not to violate the pact of Misenum, and threatening Menas with punishment as

The Sicilian theatre of operations during Octavian's campaign against Sextus Pompey, 36 BC

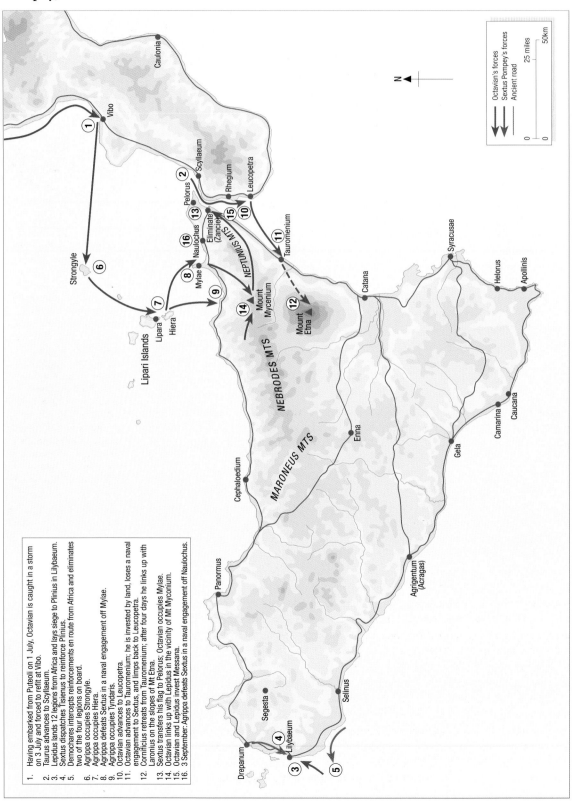

1. Having embarked from Puteoli on 1 July, Octavian is caught in a storm on 3 July and forced to refit at Vibo.
2. Taurus advances to Scyllaeum.
3. Lepidus lands 12 legions from Africa and lays siege to Plinius in Lilybaeum.
4. Sextus dispatches Tisienus to reinforce Plinius.
5. Demochares intercepts reinforcements en route from Africa and eliminates two of the four legions on board.
6. Agrippa occupies Strongyle.
7. Agrippa occupies Hiera.
8. Agrippa defeats Sextus in a naval engagement off Mylae.
9. Agrippa occupies Tyndaris.
10. Octavian advances to Leucopetra.
11. Octavian advances to Tauromenium; he is invested by land, loses a naval engagement to Sextus, and limps back to Leucopetra.
12. Cornificius retreats from Tauromenium; after four days he links up with Laronius on the slopes of Mt Etna.
13. Sextus transfers his flag to Pelorus; Octavian occupies Mylae.
14. Octavian links up with Lepidus in the vicinity of Mt Myconium.
15. Octavian and Lepidus invest Messana.
16. 3 September: Agrippa defeats Sextus in a naval engagement off Naulochus.

his own fugitive slave – Menas having been the slave of Pompey the Great, whose property Antony had acquired during his war with Caesar.

Undeterred, Octavian continued concentrating equipment and supplies at the ports of Brundisium and Puteoli (Pozzuoli), and ordered the infantry to march to Rhegium (Reggio), where they would rendezvous with the fleet in preparation for the crossing to Sicily. As his trusted right-hand man Marcus Agrippa was campaigning in Gaul, Octavian appointed Calvisius Sabinus as his admiral, with Menas under him, bidding them bring their squadrons from Etruria, and ordered Lucius Cornificius to lead the rest of the fleet from Ravenna to Tarentum (Taranto). The fact that both detachments of Octavian's navy were stationed so far north illustrates the extent to which Sextus had gained the upper hand at sea.

Sextus had scarcely heard of the desertion of Menas before he was alerted to the fact that Octavian was already moving against him. With hostile fleets closing on him from both sides of the Italian peninsula, he prepared to fight a holding action against Octavian at Messana (Messina) with a handful of ships, and ordered Menecrates, who of all his freedmen had been the most bitter rival of Menas, to take the bulk of the fleet and seek a decisive encounter with Calvisius.

When Calvisius and Menas encountered Menecrates off Neapolis (Naples) they retired into the bay near Cumae, where they passed the night. At daybreak, Calvisius commanding on the right, Menas the left, they drew up their fleet in the form of a crescent, as close to the coast as possible, in order to prevent Menecrates breaking through their line. This plan, undoubtedly that of Calvisius, backfired spectacularly, the ships on the left being so crowded their crews were forced to beach them and fight back as best they could from the shore. Menecrates now held the tactical as well as the numerical advantage; he was able to draw off and renew the attack as he pleased, and to rotate fresh ships into the line, while Menas was trapped, unable either to break out or withdraw.

At this moment, Menas and Menecrates came in sight of each other. Abandoning the rest of the fight, each immediately turned his ram on the other. Both ships were badly damaged in the ensuing violent collision, Menas losing his prow and Menecrates his oar-blades. Grappling irons were launched by both, and bridges for boarding were thrown from one ship to the other, binding them together in a death grip.

Casualties on both sides were already horrific when Menas was shot through the arm. The offending missile was, however, successfully removed. Menecrates was less lucky; he was struck in the thigh with a Spanish javelin, made wholly of iron with numerous barbs, which could not be easily extracted. Although incapacitated, he remained on station, encouraging his men, until his ship was taken, at which point, rather than be captured alive, he threw himself into the sea. Menas towed the captured ship to shore, but was unable to contribute anything more to the battle himself.

Calvisius fared better on the right, managing to cut off some of Menecrates' ships from the main body. When they fled he pursued them into open water. However, Menecrates' lieutenant Demochares, another of Sextus' freedmen, fell upon the remainder of Calvisius' ships, some of which escaped, while the rest were driven ashore onto the rocks and burned after being abandoned by their crews. Only the return of Calvisius prevented the annihilation of his remaining vessels.

A coin of Sextus Pompey featuring Neptune holding an aplustre and resting his foot on the prow of a galley. He is flanked by the two brothers from Catania, Anapias and Amphinomus, who according to the *Legend of the Pii Fratres* abandoned all their property during an eruption of Mt Etna and carried off their aged parents on their shoulders, the stream of lava being said to have parted and flowed aside so as not to harm them. This is an example of Sextus appealing to the heritage and traditions of Sicily as a means to forge a Sicilian national identity in support of his regime. (Classical Numismatic Group)

Sextus' fleet had enjoyed much the better of the encounter, but rather than press home the attack, the following morning Demochares, satisfied he had done enough to at least blunt this half of Octavian's pincer strategy, set sail for Sicily. When he learned Demochares had withdrawn, Calvisius patched together his ships and cautiously proceeded south, shuffling from bay to bay.

Octavian, meanwhile, had taken personal command of the fleet at Tarentum and proceeded to Rhegium to rendezvous with his army. Sextus had only 40 ships to cover the straits, but Octavian insisted on waiting for Calvisius before attempting to force a crossing.

When Demochares arrived at Messana, Sextus formally appointed him and Apollophanes, another of his freedmen, admirals in place of Menas and Menecrates. When Octavian heard of the encounter at Cumae he sailed out of the straits to meet Calvisius. As he was passing Stylis, Demochares and Apollophanes darted out of Messana and fell on his rear, pushing on to attack him all along the line. Octavian refused to make a stand, either because he feared to fight in the straits or because he remained determined not to fight without Calvisius. Adopting the same flawed strategy as Calvisius at Cumae, he ordered his fleet to hug the shore, riding at anchor and presenting their prows to the enemy.

Having thus been accorded complete freedom of action, Demochares was enabled to maintain constant pressure, rotating fresh men into combat while transferring his wounded and burned-out frontline marines to the rear. His fleet being driven piecemeal against the rocky promontories off Cape Scyllaeum, Octavian himself was forced to abandon ship. This freed Lucius Cornificius and the other squadron leaders to take the initiative. They cut their anchor cables and took the fight to the enemy, Cornificius succeeding in ramming and capturing Demochares' flagship, though Demochares himself made good his escape. This bought enough time for Octavian's battered fleet to hold out until Calvisius and Menas finally hove into sight, inducing the enemy's withdrawal into the gathering dusk.

Octavian passed an uncomfortable night rallying survivors to the signal fires lit on the heights. His efforts were nullified the following day when the worst gale in living memory blew up out of the south. Most captains, thinking that the wind would soon subside, as it usually does in the springtime, moored their ships with anchors at both landward and seaward ends, pushing each other off with poles.

Menas, as experienced as he was opportunistic, immediately shifted his ships to the open sea and moored them there, placing them at intervals with their anchor-lines slack to avoid their being stretched taut and snapping, and kept them rowing directly against the wind to maintain their positions. But most vessels, many already weakened structurally by battle damage, were driven against the rugged coast and lost, along with their crews. The following morning, the sea was choked with debris, and men, living and dead.

Octavian hastened to Vibo, dispatching messages ahead to Gaius Maecenas, deputed to represent Octavian's political interests in his absence, warning him to be on guard against civil disobedience when word of the disaster arrived in Rome, and dispersing the infantry he had with him to garrison key points on the Italian coast in anticipation of Sextus taking the initiative. But Sextus remained in his passive stance; he even allowed the remnants of Octavian's fleet (less than half of which was saved) to withdraw unmolested.

Sextus subsequently took to wearing a dark blue robe to symbolize his adoption by the sea god Neptune. He ordered Demochares to pillage the coast of Italy and sent Apollophanes to harass Africa. When the inhabitants of the Lipari Islands off the coast of Sicily proceeded to go over to Sextus, Octavian ordered them deported to Campania, where they were interned in Neapolis (Naples) for the duration of the war.

THE SECOND CLASH BETWEEN OCTAVIAN AND SEXTUS

Octavian still needed to settle with Antony, whom he summoned to another conference, this time at Tarentum, in the spring of 37 BC. Antony arrived at the head of a fleet of 300 vessels. He needed recruits for his projected Parthian campaign and hoped to exchange ships for men. But Octavian hesitated, and only the mediation of Octavia enabled a decision to be reached. Antony gave Octavian two squadrons, or 120 of the ships he had brought to Tarentum, plus an additional ten at his wife's suggestion, for service against Sextus. In return he received 1,000 troops from Octavian's praetorian guard and the commitment of 20,000 legionaries, four or five legions, for service against Parthia. Sextus was stripped of his priesthood and the consulship he was promised. Octavian would take the field against him the following year.

Nautical themes saturated the coins of Sextus Pompey, who styled himself the son of Neptune. This one features a naval trophy, symbol of victory at sea, crowned with a trident and set on an anchor, holding a prow and aplustre (the ornamental appendage of wood at the stern of a ship), with the heads of the marine monsters Scylla and Charybdis at its base. (Classical Numismatic Group)

Antony and Octavian (apparently without any input from Lepidus) also decided to renew the Triumvirate for another five years. As it had officially terminated at the end of 38 BC the extension was retroactively dated to 1 January 37 BC, meaning it would now expire at the end of 33 BC. To seal the agreement, Antony's son Antyllus was betrothed to Octavian's infant daughter Julia.

The divisions between the two rival warlords had been successfully papered over once more, but the divergent paths on which they were embarking would only create the context for an even more heightened level of tension in the future. In a harbinger of the flashpoint that would ultimately divide them irreconcilably, Antony had proceeded no farther than Corcyra (Corfu) when he sent Octavia back to Italy, and summoned queen Cleopatra VII of Egypt to meet him at Antioch.

With Antony's support, Octavian could have commenced the invasion of Sicily that summer. But rather than share command, and risk being overshadowed in victory as he had been at Philippi, Octavian allowed his colleague to go on his way.

Taking sole responsibility for the war against Sextus was a calculated risk. Octavian could not go on deriving legitimacy from his association with Caesar if he could not demonstrate his fitness to lead on his own behalf. Wits in Rome were already conflating his lack of laurels with his well-known penchant for gambling:

He's lost his fleet, and lost the battle, twice
Some day he'll win; why else keep throwing dice?

Octavian requisitioned funds to build a new fleet and acquire the slaves to man it. With Sextus' squadrons roaming at will the length of the seaboard, he needed a safe harbour in which to assemble and drill a new navy; Agrippa

constructed one by cutting a channel to connect the Lucrine Lake near Cumae in Campania (between Misenum and Puteoli) with the Tyrrhenian Sea. In this man-made lagoon preparations continued for the balance of 37 BC and into the winter of 36 BC, Agrippa training his oarsmen to row on practice benches while their ships were being fitted out.

Agrippa, conceding the advantages of speed and skill to Sextus' crews and commanders, built his strategy around brute force. He constructed a fleet that was bigger and more powerful than that of Sextus, and incorporated a technical innovation designed to maximize this advantage. Centuries earlier, Rome had negated the naval expertise of Carthage through the use of the *corvus* ('crow'), a rotating bridge that could be embedded in an enemy vessel, allowing for it to be stormed by marines. But the *corvus* was unwieldy and Rome lost many more ships during the First Punic War to bad weather than enemy action. Agrippa's genius was in designing a weapons system that could replicate the capacity of the *corvus* to immobilize an enemy without any cost in structural integrity to the wielder. The result was the *harpax* ('snatcher'), a combination harpoon and grappling iron consisting of a spar five cubits (2.25m, or 7ft 3in) long with a ring at each end. An iron hook was fastened to one of the rings, and a large number of ropes, twisted together into one cord, to the other. Fitted for use with the ballista, it would be embedded in an enemy vessel when fired, enabling the ship to be hauled in and boarded. An iron casing surrounded the spar, preventing the enemy from hacking it free.

While these preparations were under way, Menas, dissatisfied at being kept subordinate to Calvisius, defected back to Sextus, taking seven ships with him. Octavian seized upon this pretext to relieve Calvisius of command of the fleet and hand it to Agrippa.

The campaign against Sextus was scheduled to start on 1 July 36 BC. It combined overwhelming force with multiple angles of attack intended to keep the enemy garrisons off balance and incapable of mutual support. Octavian was to embark from Puteoli, Statilius Taurus would commit 102 of the ships loaned by Antony from Tarentum (the oarsmen of the remainder having perished during the winter), while Lepidus was to bring 16 legions and 500 horse from Africa.

Sextus had at most 300 warships and ten legions available to set against this formidable converging offensive. He concentrated the main body of his forces within a triangle formed by Mylae (Milazzo), Cape Faro, and Messana, entrusting the defence of Lilybaeum and the west to one legion and a considerable body of light-armed troops under Lucius Plinius Rufus.

Once again, Octavian's strategic initiatives were upset by the weather. On 3 July a terrific storm burst over Sicily and southern Italy. Taurus succeeded in returning to Tarentum, but Octavian was caught as he was passing Cape Palinurus and was forced to seek refuge in the sheltered bay of the Elea promontory. Unfortunately, the bay opened towards the west, and the south wind was succeeded by a southwester that blew all day and into the night. At dawn, Octavian was forced to confront the outcome: six of his heavy ships, and 26 lighter ones, not including a still larger number of liburnian galleys, had been destroyed, and many of the surviving vessels had sustained significant damage.

Octavian limped back into port at Vibo, but he refused to give up the initiative. Those of his sailors who survived the wreck of their ships were ordered to man the remaining 28 keels left lying empty at Tarentum and join Taurus in advancing to a new headquarters 50km (30 miles) from Vibo at Scyllaeum in the Gulf of Squillace.

Octavian could not risk another winter of inactivity and unpopularity in Rome. Moreover, if Antony were to succeed in imposing Roman arms over Parthia in the distant east while Octavian had nothing to show for two years of intensive effort against an enemy ensconced within the orbit of Rome herself, the power ratio between the two men would shift even further in Antony's favour. But the decisive factor in inducing Octavian to renew the campaign was the fortune of the third man of the Triumvirate.

Lepidus had lost a number of his transports bound for Sicily swamped or capsized in the storm on 3 July, but he had safely landed 12 legions (Paterculus describes these as being of half the usual strength), enough to blockade Plinius in Lilybaeum and overrun the western half of Sicily. There was still plenty of fight left in Sextus, however; he dispatched Tisienus Gallus to reinforce Plinius, while a convoy of reinforcements from Africa was intercepted en route by Demochares with the loss of two of the four legions embarked. With the conflict still in the balance, if Octavian postponed his intervention until the next available window in spring 35 BC, Lepidus would either have triumphed over or been defeated by Sextus; neither outcome would reflect well on Octavian.

As Octavian was refitting at Vibo, Menas, determined to defect yet again, paradoxically sought to prove his worth by inflicting as much damage as possible on Octavian's war effort. When ordered by Sextus to reconnoitre the enemy's dispositions he covered 150 nautical miles in three days' hard rowing and descended without warning on Octavian's shipyards, towing the galleys off by twos and threes, while sinking, capturing or burning the merchant vessels moored there. To consummate this demonstration of his superior seamanship, in full view of the enemy Menas deliberately ran his own ship onto a sandbank, waiting until the last moment before making good

The triumphal column the Senate voted in honour of Octavian's 'liberation' of Sicily in 36 BC must have looked like this modern equivalent in Columbus Circle, New York City.

his escape. Having made his point, he again offered his services to Octavian, who warily accepted.

By mid-August Octavian was ready to resume the assault in force. Agrippa was ordered to secure the Lipari Islands and harass the coast from Mylae to Tyndaris (Tindari). With Sextus distracted, Octavian would seize the opportunity to transport those legions anchored with Taurus via Leucopetra to Tauromenium (Taormina), link up with Lepidus advancing from the west, and fall on Messana; three legions under Gaius Carrinas at Columna Regia were to await events.

After taking possession of Strongyle, the northernmost of the Lipari Islands, Agrippa advanced to Hiera, the southernmost, which he occupied without resistance from the garrison. Intuiting that Agrippa intended to seek battle with Demochares, who had 40 ships at Mylae, Sextus dispatched Apollophanes from Messana with 45 ships and followed in person with 70 more.

Agrippa, with half of his fleet, sailed out of Hiera before dawn to engage Demochares. When he saw the fleet of Apollophanes also, and 70 more ships on the other wing, he immediately sent word to Octavian at once that Sextus was at Mylae with the greater part of his naval forces. Then he placed himself with his heavy ships in the centre, and summoned the remainder of his fleet from Hiera in all haste.

Sextus, observing from shore that his ships were being worsted in the ensuing battle, and that reinforcements were coming to Agrippa from Hiera, gave the signal for his fleet to retire in good order, advancing and retreating little by little to seek refuge among the shoals formed in the sea by river deposits. Unable to pursue, Agrippa withdrew, having sunk 30 of Sextus' vessels for the loss of only five of his own. His wisdom in having constructed a fleet intended to overpower, as opposed to outmanoeuvre, that of his opponent is validated in a vignette of Appian, who relates that Sextus praised his men for their courage in having fought against walls rather than against ships; he urged them not to lose faith in their speed, skill, and knowledge of the local waters, but also promised to make some addition to the height of his galleys. However, Sextus was unable to prevent Agrippa from seizing Tyndaris, securing Octavian a critical beachhead on the shore of Sicily.

Octavian, meanwhile, having received word that Sextus had left Messana for Mylae, sailed from Scyllaeum to Leucopetra. He was about to cross the straits to Tauromenium by night, but learning of the outcome at Mylae he changed his mind. Erroneously convinced that Sextus had been neutralized by Agrippa, he proclaimed that a victor ought not to steal his passage, but to cross with his army boldly by daylight. With the sea still clear of the enemy at dawn, he set sail with as many men as his ships could carry – three legions, 500 cavalry (without their horses) and 1,000 light-armed troops – leaving the rest to wait with Messala Corvinus at Leucopetra until the fleet could return to convoy them.

Sextus, however, suspecting Octavian's objective was Tauromenium, had left a covering force at Mylae and sailed to Messana. Octavian only became aware of this fact when his expeditionary force, still fortifying its camp, was caught off guard by the arrival of Sextus' cavalry. If his infantry and his naval force had attacked simultaneously, Sextus might have brought the war, and Octavian's career, to a premature end, but, unaware of the panic among Octavian's troops, and hesitating to begin a battle at the approach of night, he withdrew to quarters, allowing Octavian to finish the construction of his camp by torchlight.

Leaving Lucius Cornificius in command, Octavian led his fleet out to sea before first light, giving the right wing to Titinius and the left to Carisius, embarking himself on a liburnian, with which he sailed around the whole fleet, exhorting his crews to have courage. But most of his ships were lost or taken in battle, those of his men who succeeded in swimming to shore being slaughtered or taken prisoner by Sextus' cavalry. The survivors set out to reach Cornificius, who sent only his light-armed troops to assist them because he did not consider it prudent to move his disheartened legionaries against the enemy, who were, naturally, greatly encouraged by their victory at sea.

Octavian spent the greater part of the night among his small boats, in doubt whether he should go back to Cornificius through the scattered remnant of his fleet, or seek refuge with Messala at Leucopetra. In the words of Appian:

> Providence brought him to the harbour of Abala with a single armour-bearer, without friends, attendants, or slaves. His partisans brought him, shattered in body and mind, in rowboats (changing from one to another for the purpose of concealment) to Messala.

Had Sextus caught Octavian at this moment the war would have been over, but the desperate gambit succeeded. Having recovered his nerve, Octavian ordered Carinas to set sail with his three legions, wrote to Agrippa urging him to send Laronius with sufficient force to bail out Cornificius, and sent Messala to Puteoli to bring the I Legion to Vibo.

Cornificius could defend his camp, but without provisions he could not hold it; his offers of battle refused, his only option was to break out and link up with Agrippa. Having placed in the centre of his column the unarmed men who had escaped to him from the ships, he set out, harassed every step of the way by enemy cavalry and skirmishers. After four days he arrived at the arid lava flats of Mt Etna. With no option but to cross them at the height of summer, his men suffered terribly, choking on the clouds of ash kicked up by their burning feet. They were on the verge of collapse when Laronius, who had been sent by Agrippa with three legions, linked up with them. Cornificius, who was rewarded with the consulship the following year, was so proud of his achievement he was accustomed afterwards at Rome to ride home upon an elephant whenever he dined out.

Agrippa's occupation of Tyndaris enabled Octavian to build up his forces in Sicily, which quickly swelled to 21 legions, 20,000 cavalry, and more than 5,000 light-armed troops. Sextus still held Mylae and all the coastal towns from Naulochus to Pelorum, and retained control of the countryside and fortified mountain passes in the vicinity of Tauromenium (Taormina) and Mylae, enabling him to harass Octavian when he advanced from Tyndaris. But Sextus then made a critical error; assuming Agrippa was moving his fleet against him, he shifted his headquarters to Pelorus, abandoning Mylae, which Octavian occupied.

Octavian attempted to intercept Tisienus Gallus withdrawing en route from Lilybaeum to reinforce Sextus, but lost his way around Mt Myconium; caught in a heavy rain without tents, he was reduced to having his armour-bearers hold a shield over his head the whole night. Octavian finally linked up with Lepidus who had left the siege of Lilybaeum to his subordinates and marched the bulk of his army east (whether on his own initiative or in response to an appeal from Octavian is unknown), both triumvirs encamping near Messana.

There had been many skirmishes throughout Sicily, but as yet no general engagement. With Octavian's forces swarming all over his island redoubt the only option left for Sextus was to secure a decisive victory. He concentrated his naval forces against Agrippa at Naulochus where, on 3 September, under the gaze of both armies drawn up and watching from the shore, they fought.

The *harpax* now justified its inclusion in Agrippa's arsenal; Appian notes that, 'as this apparatus had never been employed before, the enemy had not provided themselves with scythe-mounted poles' with blades long enough to hack through the cables binding them to the enemy.

The outcome was decisive. Agrippa lost only three ships, while sinking 28 and capturing 135 enemy vessels. Demochares was killed in action, Apollophanes taken alive. Sextus barely escaped with 17 ships, fleeing to the harbour of Messana and thence to the east.

OCTAVIAN CONSOLIDATES THE WEST

The forces Sextus left behind at Naulochus immediately capitulated to Octavian. Those legions besieged at Messana surrendered to Lepidus, who united them with his own and attempted to buy their loyalty by letting them join with his men in sacking the town. Now with 22 legions under his command, Lepidus made his bid to reassert his rights, seizing the passes and ordering the garrisons ensconced in the towns he had occupied not to admit Octavian. But the men who had brought one civil war to an end were far from willing to start another one, least of all on behalf of Lepidus against the man who bore the name of Caesar, and Octavian had little difficulty winning them over. Lepidus, who, in the words of Paterculus, 'in the tenth year after arriving at a position of power which his life had done nothing to deserve, now deserted both by his soldiers and by fortune,' exchanged his military cloak for a dark grey garment, and, lurking in the rear of the crowd that thronged to Octavian, threw himself at his master's feet. Octavian indulged Lepidus in retaining his title as Pontifex Maximus, but divested him of triumviral authority and banished him for life to house arrest in Circeii.

Plinius surrendered Sextus' remaining garrisons, bringing the conflict to a close. As always in the civil wars, the price paid by the victor was inheriting the troops, and hence the financial burdens, of the loser. Rather than let them run wild, the men who had served under Sextus and Lepidus were inherited by Octavian, who now had an enormous force of 45 legions at his disposal and, as yet, no enemy against whom to lead them. Fortunately, the 25,000 cavalry and 40,000 auxiliaries under his command were not citizens and could be summarily dismissed, but only by exacting a punitive 1,200 talents from the Sicilian communities he had 'liberated' was Octavian able to discharge 20,000 veteran legionaries from service. He also restored 30,000 slaves to their masters, and crucified 6,000 whose masters could not be found.

Octavian celebrated an *ovatio* on his return to Rome on 13 November. Giving credit where it was due, he presented Agrippa with a personal seagreen banner, and, in a unique tribute, a naval crown (*corona navalis*), wrought of gold with the prows of ships worked into the design. Octavian, now 28 years of age, was granted tribunician sacrosanctity by a compliant

The Illyrian theatre of operations during Octavian's campaigns of 35–34 BC

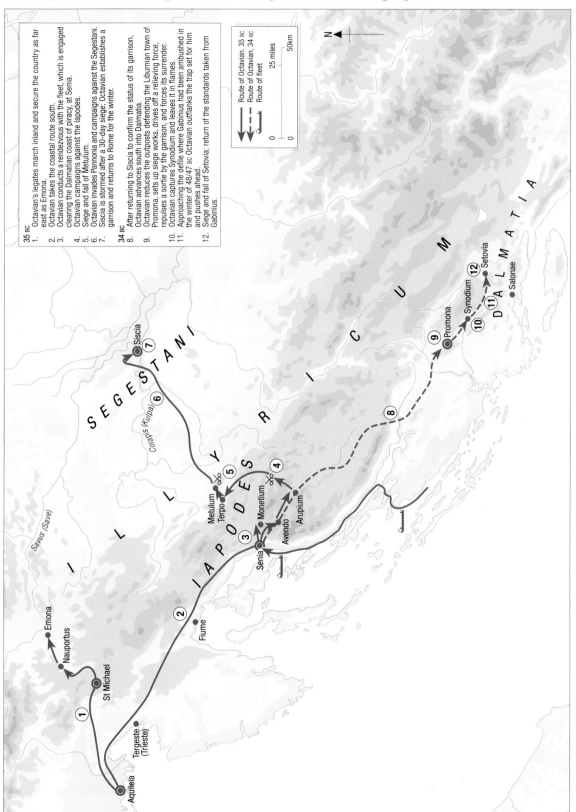

35 BC
1. Octavian's legates march inland and secure the country as far east as Emona.
2. Octavian takes the coastal route south.
3. Octavian conducts a rendezvous with the fleet, which is engaged clearing the Dalmatian coast of piracy, at Senia.
4. Octavian campaigns against the Iapodes.
5. Siege and fall of Metulum.
6. Octavian invades Pannonia and campaigns against the Segestani.
7. Siscia is stormed after a 30-day siege; Octavian establishes a garrison and returns to Rome for the winter.

34 BC
8. After returning to Siscia to confirm the status of its garrison, Octavian advances south into Dalmatia.
9. Octavian reduces the outposts defending the Liburnian town of Promona, sets up siege works, drives off a relieving force, repulses a sortie by the garrison, and forces its surrender.
10. Octavian captures Synodium and leaves it in flames.
11. Approaching the defile where Gabinius had been ambushed in the winter of 48/47 BC Octavian outflanks the trap set for him and pushes ahead.
12. Siege and fall of Setovia; return of the standards taken from Gabinius.

Route of Octavian, 35 BC
Route of Octavian, 34 BC
Route of fleet

25 miles
50km

SEGESTANI
Colapis (Kulpa)
Siscia ⑦
⑥
⑤ Metulum
Terpo
④ Monetium
③ Arupium
Avendo
Senia
Savus (Save)
Emona
Nauportus
St Michael
Fiume
Tergeste (Trieste)
Aquileia
①
②
I L L Y R I C U M
I A P O D E S
⑧
⑨ Promona
⑩ Synodium
⑪
⑫ Setovia
Salonae
D A L M A T I A

Senate, which also voted for a golden statue of him to be erected on top of a column decorated with the rams of ships, inscribed:

Peace long disturbed by discord
He restored on land and sea

This was the official end of the civil wars, a victory celebrated in *Epode IX* of Horace, who reflected the official line when he rejoiced that 'Neptune's admiral was routed and his galleys fired, although he once had threatened Rome with chains struck off his friends, our treacherous slaves.'

The final days of Sextus Pompey, meanwhile, effectively encapsulated the turbulent qualities of his character and his age. Having made good his escape, he landed at Mitylene and sent ambassadors offering his services to both Antony and the Parthians. Receiving nothing but dissembling platitudes from the former, who had intercepted his messages to the latter, Sextus seized Lampsacus, enlisting many of the Romans colonized there. Now with 200 cavalry and three legions of infantry at his command, his bid to occupy Cyzicus was repulsed, but he subsequently defeated Gaius Furnius, the governor of Asia, and seized Nicea (Iznik) and Nicomedia (Izmit).

Only when Furnius was reinforced, first by the return of the 70 ships remaining from those committed by Antony for Octavian's Sicilian campaign, then by Antony's legate Marcus Titius, who arrived from Syria with 120 additional ships and a large army, did Sextus withdraw to the interior of Bithynia, pursued by Furnius, Titius, and Amyntas, the king of Galatia. Having finally run him to ground, Titius put Sextus to death at Miletus. No doubt gleeful he had been relieved of this burden, Octavian held games in the Circus in Rome to celebrate the event, honouring Antony with a chariot in front of the rostra and statues in the Temple of Concord.

Octavian was only too happy to transfer the responsibility for the death of Sextus because, whatever the official position, the citizens of Rome mourned this squalid end to a lustrous family bloodline. Titius had survived the proscriptions of 43 BC by seeking asylum with Sextus, only defecting to Antony after the Pact of Misenum. The people never forgot his base ingratitude; many years later, when Titius sponsored a show in the theatre of Pompey the Great, the audience rose and drove him with curses and abuse from the building.

With the west pacified internally, Octavian could at last focus on meeting the challenge of an external threat. Since the borders were secure at this time, the challenge had to be manufactured. The region chosen for this exercise was the wild frontier of Illyricum, where the writ of Roman law did not extend far beyond the isolated colonies along the coast. As Dio notes, Octavian had no complaint to bring against the peoples living there, 'not having been wronged by them in any way, but he wanted both to give his soldiers practice and to support them at the expense of an alien people, for he regarded every demonstration against a weaker party as just, when it pleased the man who was their superior in arms.'

In the spring of 35 BC Octavian's legates advanced north-east from Aquileia towards Emona (Ljubljana) and the headwaters of the Save whilehe led a substantial army into the Po Valley to Tergeste (Trieste) and then marched south-east for Senia (Segna) to rendezvous with a fleet under Agrippa engaged in scouring the Dalmatian coast for Liburnian pirates. This combined force subsequently campaigned in Pannonia, overawing or subduing numerous tribes and sacking many communities, including the most significant stronghold, Siscia (Siszeg), which only fell after a 30-day siege, during which the charmed life of the turncoat Menas was finally cut short. Octavian would personally command over the course of two more campaign seasons in Illyricum to reinforce Roman authority in the region.

These exploits were hardly on the same scale as those of his adopted father, but Octavian had demonstrated the capacity to coordinate and conduct a combined-arms operation and had exhibited personal courage and leadership qualities in the process. For the first time, he had brought lustre to Roman arms in the field against a foreign enemy. He had even recovered the standards Caesar's legate Gabinius had lost in Dalmatia over the winter of 48/47 BC; the fact that as time wore on and Antony, despite his boasts of victory over Parthia, could not produce the standards lost by Crassus at Carrhae in 53 BC, contributed in no small way to a recognition of Octavian's legitimate claim to the mantle of his adopted father.

Phraates IV, King of Parthia from 37–2 BC. Whatever the chaos enveloping their Republic during its terminal period, the counter-example of autocracy as practised in Parthia should have given the citizens of Rome pause. The new king seized the throne by murdering his father and cemented his authority by liquidating, among a broad swathe of the aristocracy, all 30 of his brothers. (Courtesy Wayne Sayles)

EVENTS IN THE EAST

There is a tendency in history to retrospectively ascribe significant effects to dramatic causes. Such is the case with the love of Mark Antony for Cleopatra. Antony, consolidating his control over the east in 41 BC, had summoned the queen to meet him at Tarsus and account for her failure to support the triumvirs in the campaign at Philippi the previous year.

In Plutarch's vivid depiction of their encounter, Antony was presiding over a tribunal in the agora when Cleopatra arrived, sailing up the River Cydnus 'in a barge with gilded stern and outspread sails of purple, while oars of silver beat time to the music of flutes and fifes and harps.' Under a canopy of gold cloth, the queen lay stretched out on her couch, accoutred as the goddess of love, while beautiful young boys, like painted Cupids, stood on each side to fan her. The multitude thronged the riverbank to witness this spectacle, leaving Antony quite alone in the marketplace. His fate was sealed when Cleopatra rejected Antony's invitation to dine that evening and he, 'willing to show his good-humour and courtesy', accepted hers. The magnificent preparations, capped by a spectacular arrangement of lights, had all of Tarsus, and then the east, talking of Venus having come to feast with Bacchus. Thus, Plutarch concludes, Antony 'fell into the snare'.

The reality was far more prosaic. To begin with, Antony and Cleopatra surely already knew each other; if the dashing Roman cavalry officer and the 14-year-old princess had not become acquainted in 56 BC, when he served with the Roman force that restored her father to the throne of Egypt, then they must have done so when Cleopatra took up residence in Rome as the mistress of Caesar 11 years later.

Cleopatra's spectacular arrival and subsequent entertainments were means to an end, namely securing the independence of her kingdom. If Cleopatra had not already calculated Antony's character by personal experience, she certainly ascertained it effectively by reputation. Antony was a social animal; satisfying his desires for novelty and bonhomie ingratiated her to him, giving her enough leverage to gain his approval for acts that strengthened her authority in Egypt, for example, the murder of her sister and rival Arsinoë, who was torn from the sanctuary of the goddess Artemis at Ephesus and executed.

There is no doubt Antony enjoyed the conviviality of Cleopatra's company, both in Asia and during his subsequent sojourn in Alexandria. But when power politics intruded and the presence of Antony was required to maintain his interests he departed without a backward glance. He would not lay eyes again on the queen of Egypt, nor for the first time on the twin children, Alexander Helios and Cleopatra Selene, who were the fruit of their liaison, for another four years.

In fact, aside from an excursion to the Euphrates, Antony spent the entire period from the autumn of 39 BC to the spring of 37 BC administering his polyglot realm from Athens, apparently behaving as a model husband to Octavia, who bore him two daughters.

It was only power politics that induced Antony to again summon an audience with Cleopatra, not to revive the quasi-scandalous frivolity of Alexandria, but to address grave matters of state. Having finally resolved the nettlesome series of distractions in the west, by 37 BC he was free to focus entirely on the conquest of Parthia.

An undertaking on such a scale would require consolidation in the ranks of Rome's client states in the east. Having restored King Herod to the throne in Judea, Antony reorganized Asia Minor under strongmen loyal to him. He raised Amyntas and Archelaus as kings of Galatia and Cappadocia respectively, and reconstituted the old kingdom of Pontus from Armenia to the River Halys under Polemo.

The wealth of Egypt made it the most important of the client states, and Antony had to have its total commitment to his war effort. He and Cleopatra spent the winter of 37/36 BC in Antioch (Antakya). Early in the new year they publicly personified the common cause of Egypt with Rome in their own marriage. This was recognized in the east, but illegitimate in Rome; as a Roman citizen, Antony could not in Roman law either have two wives at once or contract a valid marriage with a foreigner. Antony had been universally recognized as the senior partner in the Triumvirate, but the spectacle of his behaving like some oriental potentate, unilaterally carving up territorial boundaries and taking an exotic queen as his bigamous bride, generated the first whispers of unease in the west.

It was true that in cementing their alliance Antony granted Cleopatra some valuable territories – Coele Syria; long stretches of the Phoenician and Palestinian coast to the River Eleutherus, the original Ptolemaic boundary, Tyre and Sidon alone remaining free cities; Cilicia Tracheia; Chalcis; Cyprus; part of Nabatean Arabia; and the fertile palm groves and balsam gardens of Jericho in Judea. The son Cleopatra bore in the autumn of 36 BC, while Antony was on campaign in Media Atropatene, was endowed with the name Ptolemy Philadelphus, to commemorate his mother's re-establishment of the Ptolemaic empire at nearly its greatest previous extent.

However, these territorial exchanges were far from representing the love tokens of a besotted admirer. The areas transferred, including Cyprus and the coastal strip, backed by Coele Syria, happened to be the chief sources of shipbuilding timber in the eastern Mediterranean. Having parted with two of his five squadrons at Tarentum, Antony deputised the task of replacing them to his client queen, who could build, equip, and man a fleet that was hers in name but at Antony's disposal.

The eastern theatre of operations during Antony's campaign against Parthia, 36 BC

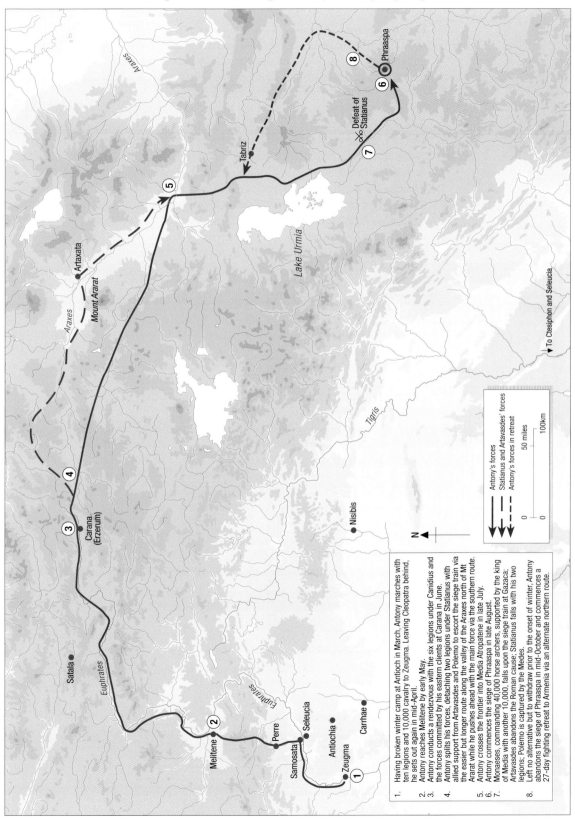

1. Having broken winter camp at Antioch in March, Antony marches with ten legions and 10,000 cavalry to Zeugma. Leaving Cleopatra behind, he sets out again in mid-April.
2. Antony reaches Melitene by early May.
3. Antony conducts a rendezvous with the six legions under Canidius and the forces committed by his eastern clients at Carana in June.
4. Antony splits his forces, detaching two legions under Statianus with allied support from Artavasdes and Polemo to escort the siege train via the easier but longer route along the valley of the Araxes north of Mt Ararat while he pushes ahead with the main force via the southern route.
5. Antony crosses the frontier into Media Atropatene in late July.
6. Antony commences the siege of Phraaspa in late August.
7. Monaeses, commanding 40,000 horse archers, supported by the king of Media with another 10,000, falls upon the siege train at Gazaca; Artavasdes abandons the Roman cause; Statianus falls with his two legions; Polemo is captured by the Medes.
8. Left no alternative but to withdraw prior to the onset of winter, Antony abandons the siege of Phraaspa in mid-October and commences a 27-day fighting retreat to Armenia via an alternate northern route.

ANTONY'S PARTHIAN CAMPAIGN

Having secured his political base, Antony was free to focus on the purely military aspects of the forthcoming campaign. The moment to avenge the debacle at Carrhae in 53 BC appeared opportune. There was dynastic strife in Parthia; after the death of crown prince Pacorus in battle, King Orodes II had designated his son Phraates his heir in 37 BC, only to be murdered by his ambitious progeny, who seized the throne as Phraates IV. The first task of the new king was to systematically purge the ranks of the Parthian nobility of any who might represent a threat to his reign. This bloodletting also served as cover for a ruse intended to sound out Antony's intentions and capabilities. It was at this time that Monaeses, the powerful Warden of the Western Marches, who owned great estates in Mesopotamia and had been designated commander-in-chief of the Parthian armed forces, arrived in Antony's camp seeking asylum. Antony welcomed his input on Parthian political and military affairs, and promised him the throne of Parthia as Rome's client king, but in spring 36 BC his guest returned home, taking with him invaluable personal insight into the physical strength and strategic objectives of the imminent Roman onslaught.

While he was personally supervising the consolidation of those states already under the sway of Rome, Antony had ordered Publius Canidius Crassus to lead six legions into the Caucasus to compel King Artavasdes of Armenia to abandon the alliance he had maintained with Parthia since the aftermath of Carrhae. Canidius then campaigned against the Iberians, defeating King Pharnabazus in battle; in an enforced alliance with this king he subsequently invaded Albania and overcame King Zober, upon whom he imposed similar obeisance to Antony.

This foundation having been established, in March 36 BC, having left Syria in the charge of Gaius Sosius, and Asia under Gaius Furnius, and having stationed seven legions in Macedonia and one at Jerusalem, Antony set out from Antioch with ten legions and 10,000 cavalry. Cleopatra accompanied him as far as Zeugma and then returned to Egypt. Antony moved on again in mid-April, arriving at Melitene (Malatya) in early May before heading north and east along the headwaters of the Euphrates to rendezvous with the other detachments of his army at Carana (Erzerum) in June. In addition to the six legions of Canidius, these included detachments led by Antony's client rulers, most prominently Artavasdes, who assembled 6,000 cavalry and 7,000 infantry under his direct command, the rest of his forces being already stationed on the frontier. The key to the ensuing campaign was an enormous siege train, including an 80ft ram, for Antony was aware he would be operating in country devoid of good timber. Antony's host numbered 100,000 men, its backbone consisting of 60,000 legionaries. Given the scale of this endeavour the absence of the 20,000 additional legionaries promised by Octavian must have seemed trivial at the time. But the dispatch of excuses in lieu of men from the west left Antony unable to garrison Armenia and thereby guarantee its loyalty.

Antony's strategic objective was to reduce the Parthian vassal kingdom of Media Atropatene. Tactical considerations dictated this choice. The direct route into Parthia led across the flat plain of Mesopotamia, ideal country for Parthian light and heavy horse. The indirect route, keeping to the rugged terrain of the highlands, was better suited to the hard-marching Roman infantry.

If the Parthians made a stand to assert their claim to Media, the Roman army would be able to fight on favourable terms; if the Parthians abandoned their vassal kingdom to its fate, Media would be incorporated into the Roman orbit to serve as the springboard for a further incursion into the Parthian heartland. In either instance, Antony's first objective would be to take Phraaspa, the capital of Media, wintering there and then renewing the campaign by marching on the Parthian capital Ecbatana (Hamadan) the following spring.

Antony's plan was to march east from Carana to the headwaters of the Araxes and Euphrates, then south-east along the far shore of Lake Urmia to Phraaspa. Antony was no doubt following the template laid down by Caesar for the abortive campaign of 44 BC, but in its execution the gulf between the two men would be cruelly exposed.

A coin of Phraates IV, depicting him enthroned and stringing the dreaded composite bow, the foundation of Parthian military power. (Courtesy Wayne Sayles)

First, Caesar would never have left his rear unsecured, while Antony had done nothing to ensure the loyalty of Armenia in his absence. Second, Caesar would never have divided his forces in hostile terrain whereas Antony, his siege train making his progress painfully slow, split his army to pass on either side of Mt Ararat. He left two legions under Oppius Statianus with the allied detachments under Artavasdes and Polemo to accompany the siege train via the easier but longer route along the valley of the Araxes while he pushed ahead with the main force.

Antony arrived before Phraaspa towards the end of August. But Monaeses, at the head of 40,000 horse archers, supported by the king of Media with another 10,000, fell upon the second column at Gazaca. Artavasdes, whose cavalry constituted the greater part of the escort for the column, abandoned the Roman cause and rode for home. The two legions, 10,000 men, fell with Statianus, Polemo was captured by the Medes, and the siege train, upon which such care had been lavished, went up in flames.

Antony refused to be daunted by this setback. Having established a line of circumvallation around Phraaspa, he ordered construction of a mound against the walls, and was able to scrape together enough timber to jerry-rig substitute siege engines. However, although doubtless establishing a line of contravallation to keep the main Parthian army at bay, the presence of such a large, mobile force established on his perimeter severely restricted Antony's options. According to Dio, 'in short, although he was supposed to be the besieger, he was enduring the hardships of the besieged.'

Antony did everything in his power to bring Monaeses to bay. On one occasion he retired a day's march from the city with ten legions, three praetorian cohorts and all of his cavalry to systematically despoil the surrounding countryside. Having drawn off a substantial Parthian force, Antony broke camp. Ostensibly leading his men back to their siege lines, in fact he had given orders the horse should charge as soon as the legions advanced near enough to second them. But the Parthian horse shadowing his movements would not stand and fight; though Antony's infantry pursued them for 10km (6 miles) and his cavalry for 20km (12 miles) more they had nothing to show for it beyond 30 prisoners taken and only 80 Parthian dead. Returning to Phraaspa the following day they had to fight their way through the main body of the Parthian army, which subjected them to incessant harassment. Having reached the security of his siege lines Antony discovered the forces entrusted to defend them had panicked and fled when the garrison had sallied against the mound, putting his improvised siege machines to the torch. He restored discipline by decimating the offending units and putting the survivors on barley instead of wheat rations.

ANTONY'S RETREAT FROM MEDIA ATROPATENE IN 37 BC (pp. 24–25)

Even 17 years after the debacle at Carrhae the Romans had still not sufficiently absorbed the lesson that a combined-arms force was required to wrest the initiative from the Parthians, especially on their home soil. Having been stripped of his cavalry by the defection of his Armenian ally, and having failed to incorporate a corps of archers, mounted or otherwise, in his expeditionary force, Antony was unable to establish any kind of perimeter to keep the Parthians at bay. His legions suffered accordingly during their retreat from Media Atropatene. Any stragglers or units that became detached from the main body would be quickly overwhelmed.

The Parthian horse archers favoured loose, baggy clothing suitable for protracted periods in the saddle, personal protection amounting to little more than a leather kaftan and simple felt cap. Their primary weapon was the powerful composite bow, which was carried, along with a plentiful supply of arrows, in the quiver (*gorytos*) slung alongside the saddle (1). Employing shoot-and-scoot tactics, they would remain outside the enemy's zone of retaliation.

On one occasion, Antony was able to set a trap for his elusive enemy and secure a rare tactical success. Under heavy fire from the Parthian horse archers while descending a hill, their shields peppered with Parthian arrows, Antony's legionaries allowed the light-armed skirmishers to withdraw into the centre of the column (2), then adopted the signature Roman defensive formation, the *testudo* (3). As described by Plutarch, 'those in the first rank knelt on one knee, holding their shields before

them, the next rank holding theirs over the first, and so again.'

The Parthians, who had never seen anything of the kind before, thought the legionaries were submitting en masse to fatigue or their wounds and were ripe for the slaughter. But, having drawn the enemy close enough to engage in hand-to-hand combat, Antony (4) sprang the trap, signalling via standard and trumpet (5) the length of the line for his men to break the *testudo*. The legionaries promptly sprang to their feet and charged down the slope (6), almost frenzied in their eagerness to at last come to grips with those who had tormented their every step since arriving before Phraaspa. The dismounted Parthian horse archers were overrun and either cut down or trampled over by the vengeful legionaries (7).

Some of the Parthian horse archers succeeded in scrambling back onto their mounts and making good their escape; one at least has the presence of mind to turn in the saddle while galloping away to fire back over his horse's rear at the charging Romans – the famous 'Parthian Shot' (8). One legionary, by boldly leaping onto his mount, has brought down a cataphract heavy cavalryman (9), a representative of the upper echelons of Parthian society who went into battle on horseback encased in heavy armour. The presence of cataphracts during the course of Antony's retreat is not explicitly attested to in the classical sources, but we do know that throughout the campaign reinforcements from their king arrived in the Parthian camp. Among these was the royal guard, indicating that Phraates IV had stretched Parthian military capacity to its limit.

By October Antony, subjected to periodic sorties by the besieged garrison and incessant raids on his increasingly far-flung foraging parties by Parthian horse archers, was forced to accept the reality that his campaign had failed.

In a bid to save face, he offered to withdraw if Parthia would concede the standards and prisoners taken at Carrhae, but the most Monaeses would concede was safe passage back to Roman territory. Antony finally gave the order to retreat; in his shame he could not face his troops, delegating Ahenobarbus to address them in his stead.

The sole break in his favour was the arrival in his camp of a deserter – by one account, a Roman survivor of Carrhae pressganged into Parthian service over the past decade and a half – who warned Antony that, Monaeses having staked out the path to Phraaspa, returning by his invasion route would be suicide. He offered to serve as a guide, advising the army to take an alternate route that led north before striking west via Tabriz for Armenia.

Antony broke camp with his men deployed in a hollow square, the baggage in the centre, lacing the intervals in the flanks and rear of his line of march with slingers and light-armed troops, and giving orders to his horse to charge and drive off the enemy as they closed, but not to follow them far as they retired. These measures minimized his losses for the first four days of the retreat, but on the fifth day Flavius Gallus, a senior officer, detached some light-infantry and cavalry and held his ground, refusing to fall back upon the main force even when the quaestor Marcus Titius, while upbraiding Gallus for leading so many brave men to their destruction, seized the standards and turned them round as a signal to withdraw. Compounding this error, when Gallus was, inevitably, cut off and surrounded, Antony's subordinates dispatched covering forces piecemeal and in inadequate numbers to his aid. By their bad management the rout would have spread through the whole army if Antony himself had not marched from the van at the head of the III legion to both rally the fugitives and face down the Parthians, deterring them from any further pursuit. Antony lost 3,000 killed in this engagement, 5,000 more being carried back to the camp wounded, among them Gallus; shot through the body with four arrows, he subsequently died.

Sensing their advantage, the Parthians, their ranks swollen by reinforcements, including the royal bodyguard, spent the night near Antony's camp, in expectation of looting his tents and baggage, which they anticipated being abandoned. But Roman discipline held, and the next morning the Parthians, convinced they were riding in to plunder rather than fight, were taken aback when they were received with a shower of missiles. The light-armed troops then withdrew between the intervals of the legions, which closed up in a *testudo* of overlapping shields, immune to arrows and able to repulse enemy incursions at close quarters.

The Parthians subsequently reverted to their harassing tactics and avoided set-piece engagements. The Roman situation worsened as famine and illness began to bite. The legionaries could find little food by foraging and besides this, with the few remaining baggage horses committed to carrying the sick and wounded, they had been forced to abandon their household implements, including the stone mortar and pestles used to grind wheat and make bread. Provisions ran so short a barley loaf sold for its weight in silver. Surrender, however, was not an option. By shooting down those who attempted to desert, the Parthians sent a clear signal that no quarter would be offered.

Desperate to shake off the pursuit, Antony resorted to a succession of night marches that finally pushed his men too far. They began to run wild,

Queen Musa, wife of Phraates IV of Parthia. (National Museum of Iran)

killing those suspected of having any money, and ransacking the baggage, including Antony's personal goods, breaking his plate and dividing the fragments amongst themselves. Assuming the commotion was the enemy inside the gates Antony lost heart and contemplated suicide. He pulled himself together only just in time to quell the disturbances. With order barely restored, day began to break, and with it the renewed Parthian assault. Once again the light-armed troops were ordered out to screen the rearguard as the fighting retreat continued. Having finally attained the last major river obstructing his line of march, Antony, drawing up the cavalry on the banks to keep the enemy at bay, first passed over the sick and wounded and then got the rest of the army across. The Parthians unstrung their bows as a mark of respect; but the Romans, in the words of Plutarch, 'not giving perfect credit to the fair words of their enemies', continued to withdraw in full battle array. Six days later they arrived at the Araxes and crossed back into Armenia.

'O, the Ten Thousand!' Antony had been heard to exclaim several times as he sought to shake off the relentless Parthian pursuit. In a march worthy of Xenophon, during the 27-day retreat from Phraaspa his force had remained intact throughout 18 separate engagements with the enemy.

Antony's first priority on reaching Armenia was to dispatch messages to Cleopatra. To assure safe passage through his realm, Antony, no doubt through gritted teeth, was forced to maintain the façade of courtesy with his erstwhile ally Artavasdes, who was in turn no doubt dismayed so many Romans had returned from Parthian territory alive.

The winter march through the snows of rugged Armenia offered little succour to the beleaguered troops, who lost another 8,000 of their number on this stage of the retreat, but once Antony was sure Artavasdes would not take the opportunity to finish what the Parthians began he pushed ahead, deputing Canidius and Ahenobarbus to command in his absence. Fearing Syria would be either in Parthian hands or in revolt, Antony had ordered Cleopatra to meet him at the obscure village of Leuke Kome between Sidon and Berytus (Beirut) on the coast. Braving the winter sea she hastened to him with stores of clothing and creature comforts for his troops.

The expedition had been a fiasco. In addition to almost all of the baggage, Antony had lost over a third of one of the finest armies ever assembled in antiquity, including over 20,000 of his irreplaceable veteran legionaries, and one can only speculate about how many of the survivors, missing toes, fingers and noses to frostbite, were never of the same fighting quality again.

THE END OF THE TRIUMVIRATE

Antony, at his lowest ebb emotionally, wintered with Cleopatra in Alexandria. Exhausted and depressed, he was subjected to the full panoply of Cleopatra's flattery, cajolery, and charm. Whether or not it was her intent to inculcate a psychosomatic attachment, from this time forward he would increasingly manifest a deep dependence on her sanction of his actions, craving her approval and reactively seeking solace in her physical presence during periods of intense stress.

Antony's account of the campaign in his dispatches to Rome falsified the reality of his situation. Although his agents kept him well informed of the actual status of affairs in the east, Octavian was happy to play along. Were the Roman people to become aware of the challenge laid down by Parthia,

The political elite of Parthian society also formed the elite corps of its military, the cataphract heavy cavalry. This entity, decimated during the occupation of Roman territory between 40 and 38 BC and then subjected to a purge of political opposition by the new king in 37 BC, played only a limited role in confronting Antony. Note the heavily armoured rider in this example from the British Museum is deploying his lance in a couched stance. Reconstructions have indicated such shock tactics did in fact predate the advent of the stirrup.

popular pressure for revenge could have left him with no choice but to dispatch the legions he had promised to Antony's aid.

Instead of the legions he had promised, Octavian sent him the 70 of his 130 ships remaining after the Sicilian campaign. Antony was only now beginning to understand Octavian was starving him of support precisely because he couldn't allow victory to a rival in the east that would overshadow his own position in Rome. In any other era, this would be considered treason, but in the Rome of the terminal Republic, it was simply good politics.

Oblivious to this reality, still devoted to the reconciliation of her brother and her husband, in March 35 BC, as soon as the navigation season opened, Octavia set sail for the east with supplies and 2,000 picked troops. But upon reaching Athens she found a curt message from Antony ordering her to send the men and *matériel* ahead but to return to Rome herself. Dutifully, she obeyed, ignoring an outraged Octavian's imprecations to abandon Antony's house. Ironically, the spectacle of her stubborn loyalty to her husband, which extended to raising his daughters by her but also his children by his former wife Fulvia, did much to turn public opinion against Antony.

To set against Octavian's 45 legions, Antony now commanded 25 legions, many of them significantly under-strength: seven in Macedonia, 15 in the east, and the three raised by Sextus. He raised five more, some consisting of volunteers from the Italian colonies, others vernacular.

That at this stage he remained focused on restoring Rome's position in the east can be confirmed by the fact he summoned from Macedonia six of the veteran legions stationed there, now the strongest he had, and replaced them with six legions of recruits.

In the spring of 35 BC Parthia and Media fell out. At the very least, this obviated the possibility of any retaliatory Parthian incursion into Roman territory. The strategic situation further brightened when the king of Media released Polemo and dispatched him to Antony with the offer of an alliance. Antony, eager for the opportunity to acquire loyal allied cavalry and archers, the absence of which had proved so costly in Parthia, immediately made preparations for a second march into the Caucasus.

In the spring of 34 BC Antony advanced into Armenia with an army of at least 16 legions. Masquerading under the pretence of upholding their alliance he seized Artavasdes and his younger sons. The eldest son, Artaxes, escaped and attempted to rally the people, but was defeated and fled to Phraates. Antony annexed the kingdom, in the process cementing relations with the king of Media by arranging the marriage of his son Alexander to the king's daughter Iotape.

Antony departed for Alexandria, leaving the legions behind under Canidius, no doubt intending to renew the campaign against Parthia the following year. With Armenia secured and Media at his side, this time the outcome would be different.

At this point Antony made his fatal error. He could not see that now was his last chance to maintain his position at Rome. If he had returned to the city with Artavasdes and his treasure in tow and staged a triumph for the conquest of Armenia, if he had publicly reconciled with Octavia, if he had personally energized his network of patronage among the elite and substantial following among the plebs – if, in other words, he had left no one in any doubt of his commitment to Roman values and the Roman state – then at the very least he could have maintained parity with his rival. The setback in Parthia notwithstanding, Antony retained the wealth of the east at his disposal and shared none of the burden Octavian carried in finessing the incessant demands for land and bonuses made by the ever-restive demobilized veterans.

Instead, Antony chose to share his victory, not with Rome, but with Egypt. At the conclusion of a triumphal procession in Alexandria – which Octavian's propaganda improved into an actual triumph, something that could only be celebrated in Rome – Antony took the lead role Cleopatra had assigned him in one of the elaborate, ritualized public events that were her forte.

For the presentation of these, the so-called Donations, Cleopatra, dressed in the habit of the goddess Isis, was seated on a golden throne on a silver platform, with lesser thrones for her children arranged at her feet.

Antony, costumed as Dionysus, formally declared Caesarion Caesar's legitimate son and joint ruler of Egypt. To Alexander Helios, who wore the dress of the Achaemenid kings and received an Armenian bodyguard, he gave as his kingdom Armenia and suzerainty over Parthia and Media Atropatene. To Ptolemy Philadelphus, who wore Macedonian dress and received a Macedonian bodyguard, he gave as his kingdom the Egyptian possessions in Syria and Cilicia and suzerainty over all the client kings and dynasts west of the Euphrates 'as far as the Hellespont'. To Cleopatra Selene, he gave as her kingdom Cyrenaica and Libya.

At the beginning of January 33 BC, Octavian entered upon his second consulship. Presiding over the senate, he delivered a speech, *de summa Republica*, in which he subjected the Donations to intense criticism. Shortly afterwards, he resigned the office and returned to take personal command of the ongoing campaign in Illyricum.

Antony fired off a letter to Octavian pointing out that first, Octavian had given no share of Sicily to Antony after subduing Sextus; second, he had withheld some of Antony's ships donated for the campaign; third, he had without consultation deposed Lepidus and appropriated his legions, revenues, and territories; finally, he had redistributed land to discharged veterans in Italy in a way that disadvantaged those adherents of Antony's. As a consequence, Antony demanded a half-share in all of Octavian's acquisitions of troops and territories, and a half-share of the recruits Octavian raised in Italy, the last point his by right in theory but in fact a dead letter since the Pact of Brundisium. Antony then departed Alexandria for the east, leading his army as far as the Araxes. It was here he received Octavian's response.

Octavian made no effort to be conciliatory. He simply ignored most of Antony's assertions, wounding the most when he contended Antony's legions had no claim on Italy since they had added Media Atropatene and Parthia to the Republic, 'by their noble efforts under their commander'.

It was at this point Antony finally concluded he could no longer reach any kind of modus vivendi with Octavian, who had sought to undermine and isolate him at every opportunity, leaving him to wither on the vine in the east. His position could never be secure while he was excluded from Italy. Octavian would resist any attempt by Antony to reassert his position in Rome. That meant there was no alternative to war. Accordingly, Antony ordered Canidius to take his 16 legions and march for Ephesus, where he would effect a rendezvous after mobilizing men, ships and supplies in Alexandria.

Sensing the oncoming confrontation, Octavian's partisans ratcheted up the invective in the ongoing propaganda war, Antony being constrained to issue a defence of his character entitled *Antony, on his Sobriety*. Though the Triumvirate formally expired at the end of 33 BC, Antony continued to use the title and assume the powers. However, determined to refute the charges of being in thrall to an oriental despot being levelled against him by Octavian, he pledged to lay down his triumviral powers within six months of his return to Rome and restore the authority of the senate and people. Recognizing that, by this stage, at least as many citizens were motivated by pecuniary self-interest as Republican scruple, Antony also proceeded to send gold in every direction, particularly to Italy and especially to Rome.

The consuls who took office in January 32 BC, Sosius and Ahenobarbus, were both partisans of Antony. In response to a harangue from Sosius, Octavian, surrounded by a personal bodyguard of friends and praetorians, promised the Senate he would provide documents confirming the justice of his cause. Before this could happen both consuls and a third of the Senate left Rome for the east.

After the return of his army from Armenia in November 33 BC Antony and Cleopatra spent the winter of 33/32 BC concentrating their forces at Ephesus, where, upon the arrival of the consuls, Antony set up a counter-Senate.

Antony sent word that all the client dynasts under his aegis were to rendezvous at Ephesus with every man at their disposal. Those potentates responding to his summons included Bocchus, king of Mauretania; Philadelphus, king of Paphlagonia; Archelaus, king of Cappadocia; Mithridates, king of Commagene; Sadalas and Rhoemetacles, kings of Thrace; and Amyntas, king of Lycaonia and Galatia. The exceptions were Polemo, who was assigned to maintain the Armenian frontier (in the absence of Canidius, Artaxes, having been restored to the throne by Phraates, had massacred every Roman colonist in the kingdom), and kings Herod of Judea and Malchus of Nabatea. At his wife's inducement, Antony ordered the former to attack the latter; thus both of Cleopatra's rivals for influence in the Levant were kept otherwise engaged in her absence.

Antony fitted out 19 legions, approximately 70,000 to 75,000 men, for the campaign, complemented by the 15,000 to 25,000 auxiliaries and 12,000 cavalry supplied by his client kings. Of his remaining 11 legions, four under

Pinarius Scarpus were stationed in Cyrenaica, three were posted in Syria under Quintus Didius, and the remaining four were left in Egypt.

Much has been made of the fact that in order to raise 30 legions for the war Antony was forced to grant Roman citizenship to those peoples of the east prepared to enlist in his cause. By implication therefore, Octavian brought a true Italian army to Actium, while Antony was at the head of a polyglot mishmash of orientalized colonists, mercenaries, and press-ganged slaves. However true that may have been of the respective fleets, in reality Antony is far more likely to have left his raw, mixed-race legions in the east and brought his veterans with him to Greece. Antony's 19 under-strength legions would therefore have roughly balanced Octavian's 16 at full strength in terms of numbers, but more importantly, any clash of arms between them would be a confrontation of Roman against Roman. The difference was that Octavian could continue to draw upon the recruiting grounds of the Latin west, while Antony could no longer replenish the ranks under his command with men of Italian stock. Octavian therefore had a vested interest in protracting the ensuing campaign, Antony in seeking an early, and decisive, victory.

Antony's assembled fleet totalled eight squadrons of 60 galleys (each with their complements of scouts, typically five to a squadron) crewed by 125,000 to 150,000 men at the oars and on deck. An armada on this scale – more than 500 combat vessels, complemented by another 300 transport ships – had never been assembled in the history of the Mediterranean.

The shadow over these proceedings was the omnipresence of Cleopatra at Antony's side. There was no doubt regarding her commitment to the cause. Besides her squadron of warships, Cleopatra supplied half of the 300 transports and probably a large force of rowers. She had undertaken to supply and pay both army and navy, draining all the carefully hoarded reserves of her kingdom into an enormous war chest of 20,000 talents. By way of comparison, a full legion cost 40 to 50 talents per annum to maintain.

But Cleopatra was not content to remain in the shadows at Alexandria and let Antony take the field on her behalf. She was determined to accompany him on the campaign, and not merely as his consort but as his partner and co-equal at the head of their combined force. This single fact fatally compromised the Antonian war effort from its inception. Having staked so much on the outcome of the confrontation with Octavian, and, having exercised executive power in her own realm for the better part of two decades, being no stranger to exercising authority over men, Cleopatra may have assumed a seat at Antony's inner circle was hers by right. If so, she was wilfully blind to the realities of the Roman world with which her collision was now inevitable.

First, the looming spectre of Cleopatra over Antony's camp was an immeasurable boon to Octavian, at a stroke confirming the perception he had been labouring to construct for months, if not years, of himself as champion of Rome's Republican heritage and Antony as the dupe of an alien queen. Second, Cleopatra's presence was like a cancer in Antony's inner circle. A poisonous legacy of Rome's Republican institutions was the total exclusion of women from the political sphere. Antony's senior officers were all steeped in this deeply misogynistic tradition and could hardly be expected to accept any woman as a coequal in councils of war, let alone a foreign monarch most of them despised personally for her undue influence over their commander-in-chief.

In April 32 BC the Antonian headquarters was transferred to Samos, and from there the passage was made to Athens in May. Octavian was content to let Antony build up his forces on the far side of the Ionian Sea unmolested for the duration of the year, all the better to reinforce the impression of the looming foreign threat to Rome, which he needed to justify his unilaterally assuming extraordinary powers for the defence of Italy. As he was neither consul for the year, nor any longer, technically, a triumvir, he had no legal basis for this authority.

Furthermore, Octavian still lacked a *casus belli*, an overt manifestation of hostility towards Rome on the part of Antony. He finally got it in June when Antony formally repudiated Octavia. Two of Antony's closest associates, Munatius Plancus and his nephew Marcus Titius, promptly defected, bringing with them a critical piece of information; Antony had deposited his will with the Vestal Virgins at Rome. Making the calculated gamble that he could ride out the backlash against violating Vestal sacrosanctity, Octavian seized the document. It was the trump card he had been waiting for. In a carefully crafted speech he then revealed to the Senate and people of Rome the extent of Antony's devotion to Cleopatra, which reached its apotheosis in the request that, even should he die in Rome, his body should be laid to rest in Alexandria.

Here at last was the proof, written in Antony's own hand, that he had fallen under the spell of the Egyptian sorceress. Octavian was now in a position to assume supra-constitutional authority. As he put it in his *Res Gestae* (his epitaph written 45 years after the event), 'All of Italy voluntarily swore allegiance to me and demanded me as leader in the war in which I was victorious at Actium: the Gallic and Spanish provinces, Africa, Sicily, and Sardinia swore the same oath.' This oath was a hybrid of the *sacramentum*, sworn by soldiers to obey their commanders and not desert the standards, and the *coniuratio*, sworn by citizens to a commander who would defend the state when rebellion threatened in Italy.

Antony was deprived of his triumviral power and of the right to take office as consul in 31 BC – being stripped, as Plutarch reports, 'of the authority which he had let a woman exercise in his place.' Octavian slandered Antony for having drunk potions that had bereaved him of his senses, and defined his rival as being in thrall to a degenerate oriental court, the guiding military lights of which were eunuchs and Cleopatra's handmaids.

Before the temple of Bellona, Octavian formally initiated the ritualized declaration of a *iustum bellum*. But, having celebrated an end to the civil wars in 36 BC, he now declared war on Cleopatra alone. The utmost care was taken to define the coming conflict on Octavian's terms: not for what it was, the showdown between two rival warlords, but as Rome vs. Egypt, Republic vs. monarchy, Latin vs. oriental, domestic deities vs. foreign gods, male vs. female, west vs. east.

The rhetoric by which Octavian legitimized his clash with Antony, and defined the significance of his victory afterwards in order to construct a cult of personality based around his status as saviour of the Roman tradition and *pater patriae*, father of his country, can be discerned from the literature composed during the Principate by those authors who personally experienced the era of civil war and reconstructed it in their poems. 'Now Romans are a woman's slaves,' Horace lamented in *Epode IX*, denigrating Cleopatra while condemning Antony, 'and at the beck and call of wrinkled eunuchs'. He invoked the full panoply of the 'Gods of my country, native heroes, and you

The Parthian army comprised swarms of mounted archers, men who had to be as skilled at retaining control of their horses as they were with the bow. This coin, issued by Titus Labienus, a renegade Roman in Parthian service, depicts a typical cavalry mount. Note the absence of stirrups and the prominent *gorytus*, acombination bow case and quiver, slung to allow easy access on the gallop. (Courtesy Wayne Sayles)

Romulus, and mother Vesta,' urging them to stand by Octavian in this crisis: 'do not prevent this young man, at least, from rescuing a ruined generation'.

The clash of arms at Actium resonates with the central theme of the *Aenead*, the foundation myth of Rome, namely its desire to define Roman identity as distinct from, and superior to, the foreign. 'Monstrous gods of every kind and barking Anubis hold weapons against Neptune and Venus, against Minerva', Virgil intones. The physical manifestation of this alien threat to Rome was 'Antony, with barbaric wealth and exotic arms… bringing with him Egypt and the strength of the Orient…and there follows – the shame! – his Egyptian wife.'

Even still, the impression created by Augustan propaganda of Italy united under the banner of Caesar's heir is illusory. Antony retained significant residual appeal among his veterans and clients, and his agents were actively disseminating throughout Rome and the provinces the apparently limitless funds at his disposal. We learn from Dio that after his victory Octavian expelled those communities that had remained steadfast in their loyalty to Antony, granting their homes and lands to his troops. Italian ardour for the war effort cooled even further when Octavian levied fresh taxes amounting to one-quarter of the annual income from all citizens and a capital levy of one-eighth on all freedmen who possessed property worth 200,000 sesterces or more. Civil unrest, rioting and arson promptly ensued that had to be subdued by armed force.

On the brink of their final trial of arms it might legitimately be asked whether the confrontation between Antony and Octavian need ever have occurred; could they not have maintained the status quo, each content to govern within the boundaries he had staked out? After all, as Syme, points out, the border between their respective spheres was 'the frontier given by nature, by history, by civilization and by language between the Latin West and the Greek East', and the partition of the Roman world into distinct western and eastern administrative units would be increasingly resorted to as an expedient before becoming formalized four centuries after Actium. But this division was only made possible by the desire to more effectively distribute the burdens of empire and by the diffusion of power into the provinces. In a still vigorous garrison state where all power remained tightly concentrated in Rome, an alternate node of political – and, by definition, military – authority could not be tolerated.

Octavian's proximate reason for provoking Antony into taking up arms against him (which, when spun by Octavian's propaganda, became taking up arms against the legacy of Caesar and Rome herself) was that he had to have the riches of the east to pay off and settle the veterans whose smouldering demands for bonuses and land threatened to erupt at any time into massive social unrest the length and breadth of Italy. There was simply nothing comparable to the revenue generating entrepôts of Asia Minor, Syria and, especially, Egypt at the western end of the Mediterranean (this endemic feature of the socio-economic milieu constructed by Rome explains why the eastern empire would survive the downfall of its counterpart in the west).

But ultimately, Octavian's political agenda had always been guided by his understanding that only one man could be first citizen, *princeps*, in Rome. Antony failed to grasp this reality until it was too late.

CHRONOLOGY

38 BC

January 17	Wedding of Octavian and Livia.
Winter	Defection of Menas hands Sardinia and Corsica to Octavian.
Spring	Abortive conference between Antony and Octavian at Brundisium.
Summer	Octavian defeated in naval engagements at Cumae and Cape Scyllaeum.

37 BC

Spring	Conference between Antony and Octavian at Tarentum.

36 BC

Winter	Canidius campaigns in the Caucasus.
March	Antony commences the Parthian campaign.
July 1	Octavian commences the Sicilian campaign .
July 3	Adverse weather forces Octavian to postpone the Sicilian campaign.
Late July	Antony crosses the frontier into Media Atropatene.
Mid-August	Renewal of the Sicilian campaign.
Late August	Antony commences the siege of Phraaspa.
September 3	Battle of Naulochus.
Mid-September	Flight of Sextus; Lepidus stages a failed insurrection against Octavian and is divested of triumviral authority.

Late October	Antony abandons the siege of Phraaspa and commences a 27-day fighting retreat to Armenia.
November 13	Octavian returns to Rome.
Winter	Antony leaves the remnant of his army in Syria and returns to Alexandria with Cleopatra.

35 BC

March	Octavia sails from Italy to join Antony; arriving at Athens she receives his order to return home.
Spring	Octavian campaigns in Illyricum.
Summer	Sextus is run to ground and executed.

34 BC

Spring	Octavian campaigns in Illyricum.
Summer	Antony conquers Armenia.
Autumn	Donations of Alexandria.

33 BC

January 1	Octavian takes office as consul for the second time; after attacking the Donations, he resigns from office.
Spring	Octavian campaigns in Illyricum.
Summer	Antony advances from Alexandria to the Araxes; receiving no redress of his grievances in his correspondence with Octavian he resolves on forcing a military confrontation to settle affairs between them.
Winter	Antony and Cleopatra mobilize their forces at Ephesus.

32 BC

January 1	Antony's partisans, Sosius and Ahenobarbus, take office as consuls; shortly afterwards they quit Rome with a quarter of the Senate to join Antony.
April	The Antonians advance to Samos.
May	The Antonians advance to Athens.
Summer	Antony formally divorces Octavia. Defection of Plancus and Titius. Octavian seizes and publicizes Antony's will. The Senate strips Antony of triumviral power and the consulship for the following year. Octavian formally declares war on Cleopatra.
Autumn	The communities of the west bound by oath to Octavian.
Winter	Antony distributes garrisons along the west coast of Greece, stations the fleet at Actium, and establishes his headquarters at Patrae.

31 BC

January 1	Octavian takes office as consul for the third time.
Spring	Agrippa seizes Methone. Octavian advances on Actium. Antony occupies Actium.
Summer	Antony's stratagems to blockade Octavian or draw him into battle fail. Agrippa seizes Leucas and Patrae.
August 29	Antony gives orders for a breakout by sea.
September 2	Battle of Actium.
September 9	Surrender of Antony's legions in Greece.
Mid/late September	Cleopatra returns to Alexandria. Octavian advances to Athens. Defection of Scarpus hands Cyrenaica to Octavian.

Winter	Octavian holds court at Samos. Defections of Amyntas, Polemo, and Archelaus hand Asia Minor to Octavian.

30 BC

January 1	Octavian takes office as consul for the fourth time.
End of January	Octavian forced to return to Italy to quell domestic disorder.
End of February	Octavian returns to Asia.
Summer	Octavian commences Egyptian campaign. Defections of Didius and Herod hand Syria and Judea to Octavian. Fall of Paraetonium in the west and Pelusium in the east.
July 31	Antony drives Octavian's advance parties from the suburbs of Alexandria.
August 1	Antony's army collapses outside Alexandria. He commits suicide.
Mid August	Suicide of Cleopatra.

29 BC

January 1	Octavian takes office as Consul for the fifth time.
August 13–15	Octavian celebrates three triumphs for his Sicilian, Illyrian and Egyptian victories.

28 BC

January 1	Octavian takes office as consul for the sixth time.

27 BC

January 1	Octavian takes office as consul for the seventh time.
January 13	Octavian feigns offering to lay down his extraordinary powers to the Senate.
January 16	The Senate confers the title Augustus upon Octavian; end of the Republic and dawn of the Imperial era.

OPPOSING COMMANDERS

A coin of Octavian, a name employed only by his enemies; from claiming his inheritance after the ides of March until his death nearly 60 years later he was always Caesar. Note the honorific 'Imp[erator]' in this early instance follows the name; by the mid-30s BC the positions would be reversed. In making the accolade a permanent attribute, Octavian implicitly signalled he was *the* imperator, a title that became hereditary with the accession of his successor Tiberius in AD 14. (Classical Numismatic Group)

Perhaps the greatest irony of the terminal Republican period is that, in an era dominated by the sword, a succession of inspired military leaders – Marius, Sulla, Pompey, Caesar – failed to impose a viable alternative to the Republican constitution. Conversely, for all the martial qualities implied in the name he bore after his adoption, **Gaius Julius Caesar Octavianus** never won a set-piece battle in his life – Hirtius was owed the laurels at Mutina in 43 BC, Antony at Philippi in 42 BC, Agrippa at Naulochus in 36 BC and Actium in 31 BC, while Antony's army simply melted away at Alexandria in 30 BC – but it was he who laid the foundations for an imperial system that dominated the Mediterranean world for centuries after his death.

The sole basis of Octavian's political legitimacy was his inheritance from Caesar, yet the two men could not have been more different in their approach to war. Caesar was bold, intuitive and impetuous, while his adopted son, according to Suetonius, 'thought nothing more derogatory to the character of an accomplished general than precipitancy and rashness.' True to the proverbs he was fond of quoting – 'Make haste slowly,' and 'The cautious captain's better than the bold' – his dominant traits were methodical preparation, dogged determination, and effective delegation.

This latter policy reflected one of Octavian's most significant personal qualities, his appreciation of his own limitations. His was the junior role in the campaign against Antony under the consul Hirtius in 43 BC, and again at Philippi, this time under Antony, the following year. He could not induce his legions to take the field against Antony during the Perusine war, and his invasion of Sicily in 38 BC was an abject failure. From this point on he came increasingly to rely on capable subordinates, primarily the faithful Agrippa.

Even so, Octavian's own contribution to the defeat of Sextus was marginal. After disembarking at Tauromenium he lost his fleet, left his army trapped, and only escaped back to the mainland with his life through the intercession of loyal subordinates. Aware that he could only earn the respect of the Roman people through being able to claim a triumph in his own name, Octavian took personal command during operations in Illyricum during 35–33 BC. The enemy had been carefully chosen for maximum propaganda value at minimum risk, but nonetheless, when called upon Octavian displayed the requisite characteristics of selfless devotion to victory, ruthlessness, and stoic virtue in the face of adversity.

During the siege of Metulum the defenders succeeded in bringing down three of the four bridges the Romans had thrown across from their siege mounds to the wall. As the attack faltered, Octavian seized a shield and, accompanied by Agrippa and just a handful of men, charged across the last bridge himself. He had almost reached the wall when the rank and file, shamed by his example, rushed after him in such numbers this bridge too collapsed, sending everyone tumbling into the fosse. Some were killed; Octavian was among the wounded, being injured in the right leg and in both arms. Ignoring the pain, he ordered the construction of new bridges, and ascended a siege tower, showing himself safe and sound to prevent false reports of his death leading to a loss of momentum in the assault.

After this incident, no doubt widely reported by Octavian's profuse and all-pervasive propaganda network, the sneering references of Antony's partisans to Octavian's seeking shelter in the swamp while his colleague won the first battle at Philippi began to sound like ancient history.

Having proved his point, Octavian was content to maintain strategic oversight of the campaign against Antony in 31 BC, assigning freedom of action at the operational level to subordinates, even going so far as to defer his own tactical dispositions on the day of battle to those of Agrippa. This ability to swallow his pride gave him the victory at Actium.

For the rest of his long reign he never took the field in person again, assigning the expansion of the empire to subordinates, usually competent (Drusus, Tiberius), occasionally not (Varus). His mantra was that a battle or a war ought never to be undertaken, unless the prospect of gain overbalanced the fear of loss, for men who pursue small advantages with no small hazard resemble those who fish with a golden hook, the loss of which, if the line should happen to break, could never be compensated by all the fish they might take.

For Octavian, military success was not an end in itself but merely a means to an end, namely, the consummation of the imperial system. He understood that basing his authority on martial prowess and the application of naked power could never succeed in reconciling the Republican diehards to his vision of a new 'partnership' in government.

Only rarely during his ascendancy did he let the mask slip, as when he convened the senate in early 32 BC having surrounded himself with a praetorian guard and friends who carried concealed daggers. Typically, his method was a subversive, not overt, undermining of Republican institutions.

In the speech of Antony that Dio reports on the eve of battle at Actium, he criticizes Octavian's adherents, 'who do not perceive that they are training a sovereign to rule over themselves.' The analysis was entirely cogent, but by that point, given the alternative, irrelevant.

Few autocrats in history have been as lucky as Octavian in having so reliable a right hand as **Marcus Vipsanius Agrippa**, a man who surpassed him in so many qualities, not least in the arts of war, and yet remained unalterably loyal. In the words of Paterculus, 'He was a man of distinguished character, unconquerable by toil, loss of sleep or danger, well disciplined in obedience, but to one man alone, yet eager to command others; in whatever he did he knew no such thing as delay, but with him action went hand in hand with conception.' Octavian's assumption of supreme power could not have occurred

Mark Antony was 52 years old in 31 BC. As he told his men on the eve of battle at Actium, 'I am at that age when men are at their very prime, both in body and in mind, and are hampered neither by the rashness of youth nor by the slackness of old age.' More salient was another personal quality: 'I have been ruled much and have ruled much.' Throughout his career his defining characteristic was his great success in the former role and his ultimate failure in the latter. (Classical Numismatic Group) without the suppression of Sextus and the defeat of Antony, and since both of those key turning points in his ascendancy were largely owed to the military prowess of Agrippa, he may be said to have been the midwife of the imperial era.

Possibly the same age (certainly, no more than a year separated them), Octavian and Agrippa were childhood friends who were studying together at Apollonia in 44 BC when they received word that Caesar had been assassinated. Rising in Octavian's service during the tempestuous period that ensued, Agrippa's status as the regime's chief lieutenant was secured after the treachery and death of Quintus Salvidienus Rufus in 40 BC.

Appointed governor of Transalpine Gaul, in 38 BC he was the second Roman commander after Caesar to lead troops across the Rhine. Returning to Rome, at the beginning of 37 BC he assumed office as consul, but refused to celebrate the triumph he was due, maintaining it would be inappropriate at such a period of crisis for Octavian. He then set to work on reducing Sicily, designing and outfitting a fleet and training its crews to his specifications, overcoming the challenge of securing a safe haven for his preparations by altering the physical geography of the Italian coastline itself. Through a prodigious feat of engineering he was able to cut through the strip of land separating Lake Lucrinus from the sea, thus forming an outer harbour, and then connect it to Lake Avernus, which served as an inner harbour.

Coin of Marcus Lepidus. Paterculus perhaps exaggerates in describing the junior partner in the Triumvirate as 'the most fickle of mankind, who had not earned the long-continued kindness of fortune through any qualities of his own,' but certainly goes too far when he labels him 'a useless partner in another's victory.' Lepidus in fact made a significant contribution to Octavian's suppression of Sextus Pompey. (American Numismatic Society)

The extent to which he or Octavian was responsible for the strategic dispositions of the Sicilian campaign of 36 BC is unknown, but his tactical initiatives were responsible for bringing Sextus to bay, and his victory at Naulochus effectively ended the war.

Agrippa was as dedicated to advancing Octavian's cause in the political arena as he was on the battlefield. The public works he sponsored in Rome as an aedile in 33 BC – new construction, repair to the extant infrastructure, theatrical performances – emphasized the commitment of Octavian to the city, as opposed to the protracted absence of Antony.

Just as he had done five years earlier, Agrippa first laid the foundation for Octavian's victory in 31 BC by a series of tactical initiatives that left Antony with no option other than seeking a decisive encounter at sea, and then won the ensuing battle at Actium.

Plutarch relates the key to **Marcus Antonius** (Mark Antony) was that 'there was much simplicity in his character,' a perspective shared by Appian, who describes him as being 'at all times of a frank, magnanimous, and unsuspecting nature.' He was a born soldier and leader of men, with the inestimable gift of being able to establish an instant rapport with the legionaries under his command. The rank and file, sensing a kindred spirit in Antony, proffered their dedicated and dogged loyalty in return.

His great flaw lay in assuming the camaraderie and bonds of mutual trust that defined life in camp applied to the universe of politics. He possessed an explosive temper but did not harbour grudges; many of the Republicans who survived Philippi gravitated into his camp, even Caesar's assassins, who could expect no such indulgence from Octavian. He was overly generous to his friends, easily bored, and highly susceptible to flattery.

All of these traits were exploited by Cleopatra, whose relationship with Antony, according to Plutarch, served 'to awaken and kindle to fury passions that as yet lay still and dormant in his nature, and to stifle and finally corrupt any elements that yet made resistance in him, of goodness and a sound judgment.'

A bust of Agrippa, housed in the archaeological museum at Nicopolis, the site of his greatest triumph.

In his *Pensées*, the philosopher Blaise Pascal asserted Cleopatra's classically beautiful profile changed world history: 'Cleopatra's nose, had it been shorter, the whole face of the world would have been changed.' In fact, as this coin indicates, Cleopatra did not conquer men by the power of her physical beauty. Her weapons were her intelligence and ambition channelled through her personality – vivacious, witty, and engaging – and her charm. 'Plato admits four sorts of flattery,' Plutarch observes, 'but she had a thousand.' (Courtesy Wayne Sayles)

Dio asserts Antony 'was characterized equally by greatness of soul and by servility of mind,' traits that made him 'a slave to the passion and the witchery of Cleopatra.' Appian, too, concludes that once Antony fell under the spell of the queen of Egypt, 'Whatever Cleopatra ordered was done, regardless of laws, human or divine.'

Modern interpretations of Antony's career continue to stress the role of his deference to, and desire for the approval of, Cleopatra. Tarn and Charlesworth represent Antony's downfall as the corollary of his passions. Two women had been devoted to him; had he followed Fulvia's lead he might have been master of the Roman world; had he remained faithful to Octavia he might have divided it. Instead he chose Cleopatra, whose only devotion to him was as the instrument of her ambition; and her he would follow, and follow to his ruin, because he loved her. 'That is what redeems his memory, that at the end he did lose half the world for love.'

In the final analysis, however, Antony was not broken in the bedchamber but at the bargaining table and on the battlefield. Simply put, Antony was a warrior, focused on short-term projects, while Octavian was a politician, able to appreciate the big picture.

Antony let every opportunity he was accorded to sponsor opposition to Octavian in the west slip through his fingers. He refused to intervene in support of his wife and brother during the Perusine War, spurned the treachery of Salvidienus, rejected any sort of accommodation with Sextus, and left Lepidus to be politically emasculated. By at least passively acquiescing in Octavian's elimination of every real or potential threat within his sphere of influence he allowed his rival to consolidate his control over the west and ultimately devote its full force to the campaign against him.

Over the final decade of his life Antony never succeeded in living up to the reputation he established at Philippi. In aspiring to execute Caesar's abortive campaign against Parthia and surpass Alexander in his conquest of the east, he had bitten off more than he could chew. Although he shared their common touch and ability to bond with the rank and file, he was never in the same league of either as a military commander at the strategic or tactical levels. Having assembled one of the finest armies in antiquity he succeeded only in leading it to a catastrophic defeat. Although he partially redeemed himself by holding his men together during their fighting retreat, he was wrong-footed at the outset of the Actium campaign and consistently outgeneralled for its duration.

Antony's key flaw was his failure of imagination. He was able to break the strategic impasse at Philippi with a succession of bold tactical initiatives because he had not committed himself to any predetermined agenda, leaving him free to extemporize, and because Brutus and Cassius, having seized the high ground, subsequently remained in a reactive posture. But, having assembled mighty hosts in 36 BC and 31 BC and defined a plan of operation intended to unfold according to a specific timetable, it never seems to have occurred to him that the enemy might not passively conform to the determinants of his strategic expectations but rather seek the initiative by taking the fight to him. Confronted with this reality, in each instance Antony typically fell back on an instinctive response – the correct one, to stay with his men, during the retreat from Phraaspa; and the wrong one, to flee with Cleopatra, in the wake of battle at Actium.

As the saying goes, so useful was she to legitimizing his regime, if Queen **Cleopatra VII Ptolemy Philopator** had never existed, Octavian would have had to invent her. In many ways, he did invent her, spinning the reality of a Greek queen whose overriding priority was the independence of her kingdom and the survival of her dynasty into an oriental succubus obsessed with the downfall of Rome.

Dio articulates this spin in a speech he puts in the mouth of Octavian himself on the eve of battle at Actium. Specifically appealing to the martial, and misogynistic, traditions of the assembled legions, he maintained that 'we who are Romans and lords of the greatest and best portion of the world should be despised and trodden under foot by an Egyptian woman is unworthy of our fathers,' who would 'grieve mightily if they should learn that we had succumbed to an accursed woman.'

Using Cleopatra as a foil was crucial to uniting the west behind Octavian's war effort. By extension, this required deliberately inflaming the most atavistic nationalistic and xenophobic stereotypes:

> Should we not be acting most disgracefully if, after surpassing all men everywhere in valour, we should then meekly bear the insults of this throng, who, oh heavens! are Alexandrians and Egyptians (what worse or what truer name could one apply to them?), who worship reptiles and beasts as gods, who embalm their own bodies to give them the semblance of immortality, who are most reckless in effrontery but most feeble in courage, and who, worst of all, are slaves to a woman and not to a man.

These were the terms by which the victor would define the stakes of the contest – Rome versus, in the words of Horace, Cleopatra and her 'polluted crew of creatures foul with lust'. The greatest achievement of the rhetorical offensive prior to Actium was its success in associating Antony with this alien and odious horde. Octavian might lament his erstwhile triumviral colleague 'has now abandoned all his ancestors' habits of life, has emulated all alien and barbaric customs, that he pays no honour to us or to the laws or to his father's gods.' But in the final analysis, Antony, 'bewitched' by the Egyptian queen, 'undertakes the war and its self-chosen dangers on her behalf against us and against his country… Therefore let no one count him a Roman, but rather an Egyptian.'

The reality is less exotic. Cleopatra conquered no man with her physical charms; Plutarch rather waspishly remarks that after Octavia was spurned by Antony, 'the Romans pitied, not so much her, as Antony himself, and more particularly those who had seen Cleopatra, whom they could report to have no way the advantage of Octavia either in youth or in beauty.' Rather, Cleopatra's trump card was the force of her personality. As Plutarch continues, 'the contact of her presence, if you lived with her, was irresistible; the attraction of her person, joining with the charm of her conversation, and the character that attended all she said or did, was something bewitching.'

Piercing the veil of Augustan propaganda, modern historians have pieced together a more balanced portrait of Cleopatra, rehabilitating her as a skilled political infighter and effective administrator, both prerequisites of viability as a monarch in the polyglot Ptolemaic realm. She certainly commanded the affection as well as respect of her people, with whom she was popular. She faced none of the endemic civil disobedience that had plagued her predecessors, and in fact the populace would have risen for her at the end had she not ordered otherwise.

Her aptitude in a strictly military capacity remains indeterminate. The only occasion during which she commanded in a combat role was leading the breakout of her squadron at Actium. Far from being a manifestation of cowardice, as alleged in the Augustan historical canon, she in fact exhibited in this instance a capacity for coolness under pressure and for critical decision-making in the heat of battle.

But in general her strategy was to co-opt a powerful warlord, a specialist in the arts of war, to serve her interests in the field. She can hardly be blamed for backing the wrong horse – any objective analyst would have concluded in the aftermath of Philippi that Antony was the strongman she was looking for, not the stripling Octavian – but her choice to bind her fate to his would lead to the downfall of both.

Cast of a portrait bust of Octavia Minor, from the Ara Pacis museum, Rome. Her beauty and fidelity epitomized Republican virtue in a post-Republican era. Antony's rejection of his idealized Roman wife for the sake of a foreign queen was a key weapon in Octavian's propaganda campaign against his erstwhile brother-in-law. (Courtesy Giovanni Dall'Orto)

OPPOSING ARMIES

The battle of Actium in 31 BC has long been recognized and celebrated for its contribution to both history and literature. It marked the final incorporation of the Greek tradition within that of the Roman, while at the same time cutting short the death throes of the Republic and providing legitimacy to the ensuing imperial regime. Syme describes its outcome as constituting 'the foundation-myth of the new order.' The romantic personalities involved have attracted the talents of poets, playwrights, and artists for over two millennia.

From the point of view of the military scientist, the significance of Actium lies in its constituting both the apogee and the end of an era in naval technology and tactics. It marked the last opportunity for the technological innovation and combat experience of the past thousand years to play out in the clash of two great fleets meeting in open water.

For centuries the peneteconter, the 'fifty-man' ship with a single bank of oars, was the standard warship of the Mediterranean. This vessel was very

Reconstruction of a ballista, the torsion spring-powered heavy missile weapon of the classical period, which could be easily modified to shoot both spherical and bolt projectiles. In the latter capacity, according to the poet Lucan, a missile 'shot by the taut whirl of the ballista' would be spent 'only after passing through more than one body.' (Vanni/Art Resource, NY)

long and slender, expensive to build, and hard to manoeuvre, especially when it integrated the great technological innovation of 9th-century BC naval warfare, the ram.

Effective use of the ram requires speed, but increased speed could only be derived from increased manpower at the oars; lengthening the peneteconter was not viable as the design was already disproportionately long and correspondingly unseaworthy. The answer lay in finding a mechanism by which to incorporate additional tiers of oars arranged vertically. The shipwrights of the classical era took naval technology to the next level with the design and construction of the trireme. A fast and manoeuvrable ship boasting three banks of oars, in the hands of a skilled crew she effectively became an extension of her ram, the entire vessel constituting a harmonized weapons system.

The resistance of a ship to motion through the water is governed by four factors: frictional resistance, form resistance, eddy resistance, and wave making. As speed increases, the crest of the bow wave will tend to raise the bow of the ship at the same time the trough of the stern wave lowers the stern. When this happens, the ship will lose trim, and an increasing percentage of its power will be needed to push it uphill. To defer this condition the vessel needed to be constructed as long and thin as possible to minimize resistance. In pursuit of the ideal frame the minimization of the hull seems to have been carried to the point where the crew constituted about a third of the total mass of the system.

In fact, by standardizing a 10:1 ratio of length to beam the classical engineers exceeded the maximum feasible tolerance for construction in wood; even though an intricate system of mortises, tenons and pegs joined the planking of the ship in such a way that stress was distributed throughout the vessel's skin, it was not safe to put a galley into the water unless it was fitted with large cables run about the ship from stem to stern and then put under heavy pressure by a windlass.

For all its unparalleled nautical prowess, the trireme symbolized a socio-political ethos that sat uncomfortably with some peoples. The city-states and kingdoms of the Mediterranean were defined by two distinct trajectories of social evolution. Some, like Athens and Rhodes, were oriented towards the sea, while others, like Sparta and Macedon, were shaped by a continental mindset.

The would-be heirs to Alexander the Great sought to reorient naval warfare around the missile technology and hand-to-hand combat they were proficient with on land. The trireme was ill suited to either purpose. The

vessel was so finely balanced she carried a minimal complement of marines, who were trained to throw javelins from a sitting, or even prone, position to minimize instability.

A larger class of warship was required to provide the fighting platform envisaged. However, three was the structural limit of the tiers of oars feasible in the galley template. Additional power could only be generated by putting additional rowers at the available oars.

Accordingly, a new generation of galley, the '4' and '5', emerged at the turn of the 5th-century BC. The '6' emerged mid-century and became prominent during the wars of the Diodochi after the death of Alexander the Great. These vessels were classified according to the number of rowers to each side, not oars. By the end of the century Demetrius Poliorcetes ('the Besieger', 337–283 BC) had incorporated every class up to a '16' in his fleet. In addition to a host of smaller craft, the fleet of Ptolemy II Philadelphus (r. 283–246 BC) included seventeen of the '5' class, five of the '6' class, thirty-seven of the '7' class, thirty of the '9' class, fourteen of the '11' class, two of the '12' class, four of the '13' class, one of the '20' class, and two of the '30' class. These vessels, which bore the most powerful naval siege unit of all time, guaranteed the king access to the far-flung coastal cities of his empire.

The trend peaked at the end of the 3rd century BC when Ptolemy IV Philopator (r. 221–204 BC) ordered construction of a '40'. Modern reconstructions assume she was a monstrous catamaran, consisting of two hulls, with four rudders. The minimum estimate of her length, 129.5m, is substantially longer than any man-of-war of the 19th century and surpasses even the treasure ships of 15th-century China. Her crew included 2,850 marines, 400 deckhands, and more than 4,000 oarsmen. Her sole purpose was to serve as a physical manifestation of the power of the Ptolemaic dynasty. She was far too unwieldy to serve in a combat role; the flagship of Philip V of Macedon (r. 221–179 BC), a comparatively modest '16', was described by Livy as being 'of almost unmanageable size'.

Rome emerged and expanded initially as a continental power but, although deriving her identity and military prowess from her small farmer peasant class, the consummation of her imperial ambitions ultimately necessitated taking to the water. Because the political structure in Rome was effectively synonymous with her war machine, the fleet emerged as a legitimate *locus* for the manifestation of authority. For example, the 4th-century BC Rostra Veteres, the speaker's platform in the Comitium (the space within the Forum dedicated to political debate), affixed to its façade the rams

TOP LEFT
The marines in this relief of a galley are wearing helmets and carry shields for protection but do not wear armour. Their principal weapon is the javelin; great quantities of projectile weapons would be stockpiled on deck for use in combat. The vessel is *cataphract* (enclosed); note the overlapping shield motif. (C.M. Dixon/Ancient Art & Architecture Collection Ltd)

TOP RIGHT
Ballistae mounted amidships, from Trajan's Column at Mainz. Full-scale naval engagements were already ancient history by the beginning of the 2nd century AD, by which time the once volatile Mediterranean was the placid *Mare Nostrum*. The vessel depicted is in service with Rome's brown water navy, offering fire support to those legions patrolling or crossing the Rhine or Danube frontiers. (Erik de Wagt)

A fresco from the Temple of Isis, Pompeii, showing two galleys at sea, fore on the left, aft on the right. Vessels like this may have been on station at the naval base of Misenum in AD 79 and participated in the rescue mission launched by the *praefect*, the elder Pliny, when Mt Vesuvius erupted. (C.M. Dixon/Ancient Art & Architecture Collection Ltd)

of six warships taken as spoils from the Volscians, an Italian tribe who held the coastal city of Antium.

From the beginning, Rome endorsed a tactical doctrine that emphasized coming to grips with the enemy over prowess with the ram. Lucan, in his description of the naval encounter off Massilia (Marseilles) in 49 BC, neatly encapsulates the different fighting styles:

> Whereas the Greeks' vessels were ready to provoke battle
> and resort to flight, to break off their course with no long
> circle and to respond to the guiding helm with no delay,
> yet the Roman ship was more sure to offer a steady
> vessel, valuable for warriors like dry land…

A '3' of the 5th-century had a total complement of 200 men, the vast majority of whom (i.e. the 170 oarsmen) served below decks. Stationed above decks were a helmsman with an aft deck crew of five; the bow officer with a forward deck gang of five; the rowing master; the purser; the shipwright; the piper; and a marine detachment comprised of a mere 10 hoplites and four archers.

The '4' (which had two banks of oars with two men to an oar) probably had a total of 232 rowers; the '5' (three banks of oars manned at a 1:2:2 ratio) 286 rowers. At approximately 100 tonnes, the displacement of a '5' was double that of a '3', enabling her to commit more than 70 additional marines to a combat role. Their presence, together with a strengthened deck, would have added roughly 10 tonnes in topweight and raised the centre of gravity by 0.4m, halving the vessel's stability. To compensate, the breadth on the waterline was increased from 3.6m to over 5m; further drag was imposed by the enlarged waterline wale, which accorded greater protection against ramming attacks.

The ship would therefore be slower, but the broader beam allowed for greater buoyancy and accommodated the two extra files of oarsmen on each side of the ship, enabling her to make up some of that loss by adding oar power. The top speed of a '5', 7.7 knots, compared with the 9.5 knots of the '3', could be maintained for about 20 minutes before the oarsmen would be completely exhausted.

Other factors specific to a particular vessel might place additional strain on performance. Rather like modern AFVs, galleys could be 'up-armoured' by their crews for additional protection. In his account of the clash at Actium, Plutarch describes the hulls of Antony's ships as being reinforced with great squared pieces of timber, fastened together with iron bolts, and bristling with brass spikes.

A galley's sails were collapsible, enabling them to be lowered and stowed on deck or, ideally, detached entirely and stacked on shore prior to combat. Also collapsible were the towers (*propugnacula*) that endowed a galley with greater height and range for missile attacks. Silius Italicus, in his account of a Roman galley of the Second Punic War, describes her as having 'eight towers as big as her beam allowed, two in the prow, the same number in the stern, and the remaining four amidships. Each of these was equipped with two spars to which were rigged containers by means of which stones were dropped onto enemies passing beneath. Each tower was manned by four young armed men and two archers. The whole space inside the towers was full of stones and missiles.' The larger classes of vessel that entered service during the terminal Republic had broader beams and hence could support bigger towers, with more fighting men (*propugnatores*) and projectile weapons.

This latter factor necessitated a corresponding expansion in the defensive array of the galley as it entered combat. In the past, vertical screens and light wooden canopies had been deemed sufficient protection from missiles for oarsmen, but with the increased emphasis on the exchange of long-range missile fire, the oar decks of capital ships were now fully enclosed (*cataphract*), as opposed to the open (*aphract*) superstructure of the '3' and other light vessels.

In addition to contributing to the greater overall weight of the vessel, this boxing-in imposed a further burden on the oar crews. Adequate ventilation was a critical factor in maintaining performance; even with the incorporation of detachable gratings or louvres, operating in an enclosed environment placed correspondingly greater stress on every man at the oars. This in turn exposed the limitations of the galley design in terms of carrying capacity; 10 to 15 tonnes was the maximum quantity of water that could be brought onboard a '5', barely enough to meet the daily requirement of up to four litres per oarsman.

When under sail the oarsmen had no place to sit except crammed at their benches with perhaps a metre of legroom. It was because of this crowding, the necessity to maintain adequate hygiene, and the lack of storage space for food and water, not because of any inability to navigate across the open sea, that ancient warships almost always hugged the shore, beaching at night.

LOGISTICS AND TACTICS

A Roman fleet of the terminal Republic was divided into two classes of capital ships: *maioris formae* ('5' and above) and *minoris formae*, the smallest of which was the liburnian. The figures cited for the total number of vessels constituting a fleet refer only to these ships of the line, and do not include the host of support vessels (*actuaria*) literally swarming about the capital ships. These included the stand-alone scouts (*speculatoriae*), and the longboats (*scaphae*) attached to the capital ships, which served as tenders and shuttles generally and in an emergency search-and-rescue role during combat; Appian relates that during the battle of Mylae in 36 BC, whenever one of Sextus' galleys was overpowered its crew leapt into the sea, to be picked up by longboats that were hovering around for this purpose.

The regular formation of a fleet in transit, or in the first stage of an engagement, was in column under sail or oar. The preliminary, vulnerable, movement off a beach was to form up as quickly as possible into the defensive formation of line abreast, in as many as four lines deep, before turning 'to the wing' into column ahead with either the right or left wing leading. Normally the right wing led with the commander at its head and the left wing formed the rearguard. The column (*agmen*) might again be of up to four files. The fleet would typically proceed by following the coastline, under sail if the wind was favourable.

When the enemy was sighted or, if out of sight, signalled from vantage points ashore or by scouts sent ahead, the first order to a fleet under sail was usually to furl sails and strike masts and yards. The column then moved under oar into lines abreast (*acies*) with the ships deployed to the left or right of the commander at right angles to the line of advance.

This operation was not easily carried out by a fleet hugging the shore since the commander had to leave the correct amount of space for his ships to occupy in as many ranks deep as the column had files. If he was too far out a gap formed between the left wing and the shore, and if he was too close inshore, there would not be enough room for his ships to form a line abreast without confusion. In most instances, the fleet would change from lines ahead into lines abreast by a series of turns in succession followed by turns together.

Manoeuvres on this scale would require impeccable judgement on the part of each captain (*navium magistri*) and helmsman (*gubernator*) and their maintenance of a sensitive and responsive command structure throughout the crew (*socii navales*) above and below decks. Effective coordination of the oars was critical to maximizing performance. This was particularly important in vessels of class '5' or higher, which faced the additional challenge of synchronizing oars of different lengths. The officer assigned to this task was the *hortatory*. In describing his role, Silius Italicus notes 'there stands in the middle of the stern's extremity one who with his voice regulates the alternate strokes of the oarsmen.' These strokes would be harmonized by the music of the piper; in the words of Plutarch, 'there was a beat in a certain rhythm as the oars were recovered which kept time with the periods of the flute music.'

A naval battle between two fleets of ships in roughly the same class would typically begin with a head-on clash. The vessels would close at top speed, aiming at the prow of the ship opposite them in line, all the while the marines and gun crews above decks exchanging missile fire. If neither ship secured an advantage from this initial collision they would back-water and charge again.

A fleet consisting of smaller or more manoeuvrable vessels would have a number of tactical options available in lieu of a direct confrontation. The most basic, the *periplous*, simply involved one fleet outflanking the other on one or both sides. The *diekplous* was the real test of the skill and coordination onboard the attacking galleys, which would commence when they formed up in column rather than line. The lead ship would single out one vessel in the enemy's line opposite, altering course to veer past its prow at the last moment prior to impact. The galleys following up would exploit this breakthrough, disrupting the enemy's tactical dispositions by isolating and eliminating individual targets.

A preferred means of taking an enemy ship out of the battle was by destroying its oars. Ideally, the attacking vessel would approach its victim at an angle of 20° to 40° off her bow or stern, ship the oars on the engaged side, and drive hard ahead with the oars on the other side when the *epotis*, the beams protruding from the bow, was nearly in contact with the victim's outrigger. The unbalanced oar thrust from the oars on one side of the ship would provide a turning movement that would just about balance that from the oar-breaking force acting on the stem. Once clear of their now crippled

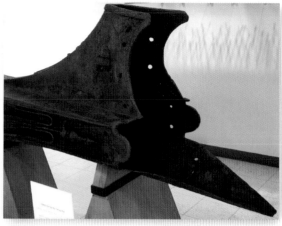

TOP LEFT
This ram, once fitted to a late-3rd-century BC galley, was found in 1980 off the coast of Israel at Athlit and is currently on display in the National Maritime Museum, Haifa.

TOP RIGHT
A rear view of the Athlit ram, showing the fitting required to secure it to the galley. The timbers incorporated within the hollowed-out section of the ram performed a vital shock-absorption role, enabling the attacking vessel to transfer the full force of the impact to its victim and not transfer it back through its own hull.

BELOW
The marines stationed onboard the galleys Cleopatra committed to the Antonian war effort would have approximated these Ptolemaic troops depicted in the turn of the 1st century BC Nile Mosaic of Palestrina.

enemy, the attacking vessel could turn about with the ram and execute an *anastrophe*, destroying the two steering oars, thereby leaving the enemy totally immobilized and easy prey.

MISSILE WEAPONS

The effectiveness of missile weapons when deployed onboard a naval vessel was compromised by two factors. First, the ballista and catapult could not ordinarily be fired at angles below the horizontal, which meant a zone of partial safety surrounded a large galley for those ships small enough to creep in close.

The second limitation was inherent to the structural imperatives required to meet the demand for the least possible wave resistance. The high length-to-beam ratio of ancient galleys made them as much as 50 times more sensitive to rolling than to pitching. Since missile firing at any appreciable range requires elevating the weapon, the head of a bolt aimed straight ahead would be farther from the ship's centre of rotation than the butt. A projectile fired after a ship rolled only slightly off the vertical would fly wide of the mark; hence the effectiveness of missile fire must have been significantly reduced when the crew aimed more or less directly ahead, for example, at a target they were also attempting to ram.

Conversely, the effectiveness of missile fire from the targeted galley would be enhanced both by its own relative stability and by the shape of the oncoming

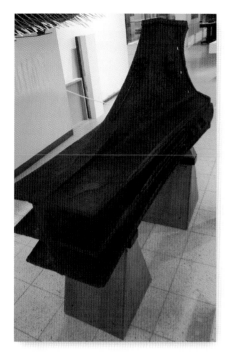

enemy vessel. The projectiles of the targeted galley, fired more or less broadside, would undergo considerable dispersion in elevation, which would translate into a 'footprint' or pattern of impacts in the shape of an elongated ellipse, a good match for the long and thin profile of the attacking galley. The echelon arrangement of the rowers inside the hull of the attacking ship would in turn increase the chances that more than one might be injured or killed by a single hit.

In contrast, the rolling of the attacking ship would cause considerable lateral dispersion of its projectiles, since it would be firing more or less straight ahead. The small depth of the target would mean that even minor changes in elevation could make the projectiles fall long or short.

Missile fire between ships was therefore more effective in a defensive than offensive mode, but given the limitations of weapon and ship construction technology it remained ancillary, not decisive, in shaping the outcome of battle. It was only when the offensive capability of gunpowder was successfully coupled with the galleon, a ship design of sufficient size to bear the weight of massed cannons and with a rigging enabling independent power under sail, that admirals would seek to 'cross the T' of an enemy fleet, deliberately offering their broadside to maximize firepower against oncoming vessels. Until the defeat of the Spanish Armada conclusively proved otherwise, closing head-on to ram and board remained the definitive tactic of naval warfare.

RAMMING AND BOARDING

The first rams tapered to a point. Late in the 7th century a new design became standard, ending in a blunt face that resembled a boar's snout, designed not to penetrate the enemy's hull but rather to deliver a pounding blow that would cause its seams to open up.

During the Peloponnesian Wars the definitive form of the ram made its debut, the warhead consisting of three horizontal fins crossed down the centre by a solid vertical section. This was designed to deliver a pounding blow that concentrated enormous forces into a very small contact area, but which was prevented by a sufficiently widespread grid from penetrating too far into the hull.

Finned rams were designed to cut into planking and longitudinal timbers along their grain, and to do so at large angles from the athwartships direction so that penetration could be achieved over a wide range of angles of attack. Ancient hulls were constructed of strakes tightly connected to each other with closely set mortise-and-tenon joints. A blow from a finned ram would therefore open up seams extending metres away from the point of impact.

The timber structure behind the casting was as important as the casting itself. Upon impact, that structure had not only to sustain a large compressive force, of the order of the ship's mass, between the casting and the main mass of the ship, but also substantial lateral and vertical pressure. Accordingly, there is evidence that the ram was a structure wholly external to the ship proper, in order that, in the very real eventuality of the ram being torn off, the attacker would not then necessarily be holed forward and flooded.

Rams varied substantially in size to correspond with the class of warship to which they were attached. The best-preserved example of a finned ram is a bronze casting from a 2nd-century galley found in 1980 off the coast of Israel at Athlit and currently on display at the naval museum in Haifa. Its weight, 0.465 tonnes, places it near the centre of a broad range of combat types. The Deutsches Schiffahrtsmuseum in Bremerhaven, Germany, is in possession of a ram weighing only 53 kg, less than one-eighth the weight of the Athlit ram. It must have come from a very small class of ship, a '2', or even a '1'. By contrast, excavations of Octavian's victory monument at Actium have revealed it was intended to display rams taken from the larger vessels in Antony's fleet that weighed up to 2 tonnes.

The key to a successful ramming attack was timing. Judging the exact moment when to back-water and slow the momentum of the attack was just as important as correctly estimating the speed and trajectory of the respective galleys once the attacking ship had targeted the enemy vessel. At the battle of Chios (201 BC), Polybius relates that the flagship of Philip V of Macedon, a '10', accidentally rammed one of her own ships when it strayed across her path, 'and giving her a powerful blow in the middle of the oarbox, well above the waterline, stuck fast, since the helmsman had been unable in time to check or reverse the ship's momentum.' Trapped, the flagship was put out of action by two enemy class '5' ships, which rammed her below the waterline on each side.

The speed of the attacking ship needed to be only 2 to 3 knots if it struck its target amidships, i.e. at a 45° angle. The upper limit of the speed required to carry out a ramming attack increased as the angle sharpened, from 4 knots at 60° to 5 knots at 45° and 8 knots at 30°. From this analysis it appears that attacks on the quarter (following, for example, a *diekplous* or *periplous*) were tactics for faster, and therefore smaller, ships. We may conclude, therefore, that a fleet of the terminal Republic period would ideally be made up of a mixed force, with larger vessels to hold the line, and smaller ones to seek the enemy's flanks and rear.

The Rhodians, specialists at ram tactics, compensated for the increased protection at the waterline by moving enough men forward to enable trimming down at the bow just before impact, facilitating penetration below the waterline. It was an effective tactic in that a hole below the waterline will cause quicker flooding than a hole of the same size above the waterline.

Even with the range of weapons and tactics available, other than by burning her to the waterline, actually sinking an enemy vessel remained surprisingly uncommon. In his account of naval combat during the Peloponnesian Wars, Thucydides refers to ships having been knocked out of action (*diaphtheirein*) or left awash (*katadyein*) rather than simply disappearing beneath the waves.

The amount of water entering the ship through an idealized rectangular hole 'b' metres wide and 'h' metres deep below the waterline would be approximately 100 b ($h^{3/2}$) tonnes per minute. For example, if the hole was 0.33 sq m below the waterline, water would flow into the ship at a rate of about 5 tonnes per minute. But this would eventually stabilize at a level insufficient to overcome the natural buoyancy of the hull, roughly 40 per cent of its weight. Instead, as more water flooded onboard, the stricken ship would settle in the water, making the oars less effective and the ship less manoeuvrable and more crank, heeling over noticeably if those onboard moved athwartships. Eventually, when completely bilged and lying waterlogged, she would be quite immobilized, and exposed to severe strain in any appreciable swell. Taking her as a prize before rough weather finished what the ram began was therefore an imperative.

Deploying sufficient marines to board an enemy vessel was problematic because this mass of men assembled towards one side of the bows would cause the attacking vessel to heel by as much as 3° and thus risk hindering the oar crew at a critical moment. Standard practice may therefore have been for troops to remain centred on the ship's middle line until springing towards the target at the last moment before contact was made.

Naval power faded alongside Republican virtue in the aftermath of Actium. Under Augustus and his successors the navy was reduced, both in its role – serving to convoy the army on campaign, bear officials and dispatches, suppress piracy, and patrol the Rhine and Danube rivers established as the imperial frontiers – and, correspondingly, in the size of the vessels incorporated, with liburnians becoming standardized over time as the generic warship of the empire. Only one significant naval engagement took place during the four centuries after the death of Augustus, and it was an internal affair, Constantine's son Crispus defeating the fleet of Licinius in the battle of the Hellespont in AD 324. It was only with the collapse of the western empire in the 5th century that naval power again became salient and a new generation of galleys emerged to contest control of the Mediterranean.

THE APPROACH TO ACTIUM

Antony embarked his host for western Greece in late spring 32 BC. There were some minor defections in his rear; Sparta under Eurycles, whose father Antony had ordered to be executed for piracy, declared for Octavian, as did Lappa (Argyroupoli) and Cydonia (Khania) in Crete, and during the winter, Berytus revolted against Cleopatra.

It was already late autumn when Antony reached the coast of the Ionian Sea, his western frontier. Having encountered off Corcyra (Corfu) an advance detachment of scouts sent to reconnoitre his position, he withdrew to the Peloponnese and went into winter quarters at Patrae (Patras), distributing squadrons of ships and garrisons along a string of islands and outposts covering the approaches to Greece. His northernmost detachment was stationed at Corcyra, which had been Pompey's southernmost outpost in 48 BC. The bulk of his fleet was laid up for the winter in the Gulf of Ambracia, the security from the elements proffered by its marvellous natural harbour complemented by two guard towers constructed on either side of the narrow strait connecting it with the open sea – one at Parginosuala Point at the tip of the northern peninsula, the other at Cape Scylla at the tip of the southern

Although descended from a purely Greek line, as queen of Egypt Cleopatra was obligated to embody the traditions and culture of her subject peoples. Here she is depicted at left on the rear exterior wall of the Temple of Hathor at the Dendera complex making ritual obeisance to the ancient gods of Egypt with her firstborn son, Ptolemy XV Philopator Philometor Caesar, commonly refered to by his diminutive, Caesarion.

The Balkans during the Actium campaign of 31 BC

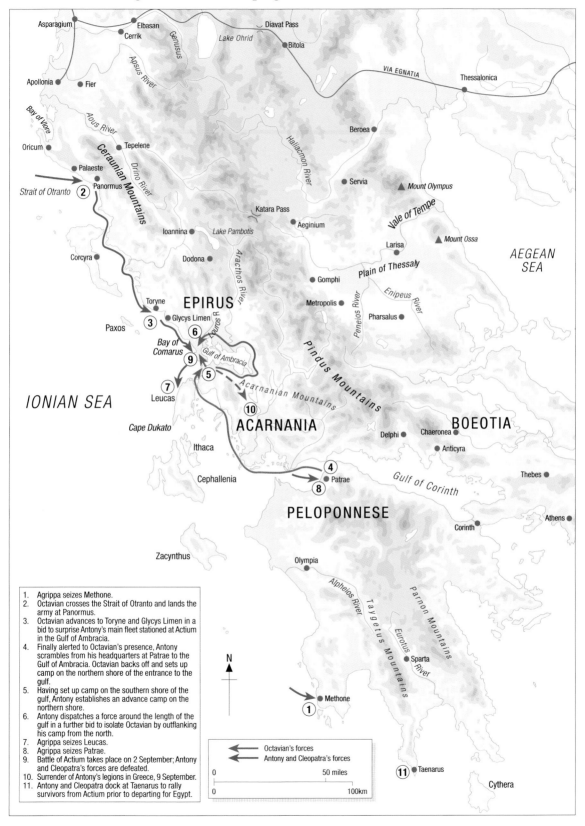

Asparagium
Elbasan
Cerrik
Diavat Pass
Genusus
Lake Ohrid
Bitola
VIA EGNATIA
Thessalonica
Apollonia
Fier
Apsus River
Bay of Vlore
Aous River
Beroea
Oricum
Tepelene
Drino River
Servia
▲ *Mount Olympus*
Palaeste
Ceraunian Mountains
Panormus
(2)
Strait of Otranto
Katara Pass
Aeginium
Haliacmon River
Vale of Tempe
Ioannina
Lake Pambotis
Larisa
▲ *Mount Ossa*
Corcyra
Dodona
Aracthos River
Plain of Thessaly
AEGEAN SEA
Gomphi
Toryne
Metropolis
Peneios River
Enipeus River
EPIRUS
(3)
Glycys Limen
Pharsalus
(6)
Paxos
Louros R.
Bay of Comarus
Gulf of Ambracia
(9)
(5)
Pindus Mountains
(7)
Leucas
Acarnanian Mountains
IONIAN SEA
Cape Dukato
(10)
ACARNANIA
Delphi
Chaeronea
BOEOTIA
Ithaca
Anticyra
Cephallenia
(4)
Patrae
Thebes
(8)
Gulf of Corinth
PELOPONNESE
Athens
Zacynthus
Corinth
Olympia
Alpheios River
Parnon Mountains
Taygetus Mountains
Eurotas River
N
▲
Sparta
Methone
(1)
Taenarus
(11)
Cythera

1. Agrippa seizes Methone.
2. Octavian crosses the Strait of Otranto and lands the army at Panormus.
3. Octavian advances to Toryne and Glycys Limen in a bid to surprise Antony's main fleet stationed at Actium in the Gulf of Ambracia.
4. Finally alerted to Octavian's presence, Antony scrambles from his headquarters at Patrae to the Gulf of Ambracia. Octavian backs off and sets up camp on the northern shore of the entrance to the gulf.
5. Having set up camp on the southern shore of the gulf, Antony establishes an advance camp on the northern shore.
6. Antony dispatches a force around the length of the gulf in a further bid to isolate Octavian by outflanking his camp from the north.
7. Agrippa seizes Leucas.
8. Agrippa seizes Patrae.
9. Battle of Actium takes place on 2 September; Antony and Cleopatra's forces are defeated.
10. Surrender of Antony's legions in Greece, 9 September.
11. Antony and Cleopatra dock at Taenarus to rally survivors from Actium prior to departing for Egypt.

⟵ Octavian's forces
⟵ Antony and Cleopatra's forces

0   50 miles
0   100km

LEFT

Obverse of a coin of King Herod of Judea. Herod, who reigned from 37 to 4 BC, owed his throne to Rome, specifically to Antony. In return, Herod was prepared to play the role of the dutiful client – up to a point. His bitter rivalry with Cleopatra complicated Antony's ambition to maintain harmony among his client rulers and unify the east under his banner. (American Numismatic Society)

RIGHT

The sacred implements displayed on this coin of King Herod manifest the insecure basis of his authority. Despite a lifetime spent emphasizing his Judaic credentials, which culminated in his expansion of the Second Temple to its definitive form, his reign was never accepted as legitimate by many of his subject peoples because his heritage was Idumaean, Jewish by conversion not blood. Such conflicting doctrinal and ethnic loyalties, not to mention incompatible personalities, made governing the Holy Land an endemic headache for Rome. (American Numismatic Society)

peninsula. A naval squadron secured Leucas and the passage inshore of Ithaca and Cephallenia to the mouth of the Gulf of Corinth. Zacynthos was held by Antony's legate Sosius, Methone (Methoni) by Bogud of the royal house of Mauretania, driven into exile by his brother Bocchus, a partisan of Octavian. Another garrison occupied the peninsula of Teanarum at the southern end of the chain. The primary purpose of these dispositions was to safeguard the lifeline of the Antonian war effort, the convoys of supply ships running from Egypt to the Gulf of Ambracia.

At first glance, it seems unclear why a veteran warrior like Antony, who had served under Caesar in the Balkans campaign of 48 BC, would simply concede the Via Egnatia, the highway linking Macedonia with the east. His strategic initiatives can only be interpreted as inherently reactive and defensive, the priority being to secure Egypt, not to carry the war to the enemy.

The reality was that Antony's options were limited, this being the inevitable corollary of his alliance with Cleopatra. Pre-emptively spearheading an invasion of Italy would only result in rallying the entire peninsula behind Octavian and against the foreign queen. His only viable alternative was to drag out the campaign, banking on Octavian's strained financial situation leading to the collapse of his position and forcing him to come to terms. Rather than take the fight to Octavian, in other words, he must make Octavian come to him. Hence the surrender of the Via Egnatia, an invitation made even more explicit when Antony withdrew his garrison from Corcyra midwinter, leaving open the passage to Dyrrhachium (Durrës).

Being able to contest control of the sea on at least equal terms with his rival meant Octavian's strategic position was far superior to that of Caesar against Pompey in 48 BC, or his own, alongside Antony, against Brutus and Cassius six years later. But his situation was far from secure. His legions were clamouring for money and he faced a wealthy adversary inviting them to treachery. Staking everything on a single, decisive clash with Antony on land was deemed unwise. It would play to the enemy's strengths; defeat would revive memories of Antony's former lustre and Octavian's subordinate role during the campaign to avenge Caesar. Italy might be inspired to rise against him, the army to desert.

It was instead resolved to strike at Antony's navy. Agrippa would feint at the southern coast of Greece in March while Octavian with the rest of the fleet would disembark 15 legions on the coast of Epirus. This force would then proceed to the Gulf of Ambracia to surprise and burn Antony's fleet.

By the end of the year Octavian had mobilized 80,000 foot and 12,000 horse, and more than 400 warships. This was a fraction of the force available to him, and the temptation must have been to commit the full weight of his armed might to the struggle. But to transport, command, and supply such a mass of men would have risked stretching the logistical infrastructure available to him beyond its capacity. The decision was made to deliberately limit the number of men committed to the campaign, the inference being Octavian embarked with only the best and most reliable of the men available to him on board.

On New Year's Day 31 BC Octavian's constitutional position was greatly strengthened as he entered upon his third consulship. His designated colleague, Antony, having been stripped of the office the previous summer by the Senate, Messalla Corvinus was elevated in his place – a clever choice, as it further emphasized the supposed reconciliation of Republican loyalists with Octavian in common cause against the threat posed by the monstrous Cleopatra.

Octavian's arrangements for securing his rear during his absence were carefully considered. Leaving the faithful Maecenas to manage affairs in Rome, he placed Gaul under Gaius Carrinas, Spain under Calvisius Sabinus, and dispatched Cornelius Gallus to secure Africa as a counterweight to Antony's force in Cyrenaica. In addition, he ordered the entire Senate to join his expeditionary force, partly to demonstrate the collective will of the Roman people in rallying to the defence of the homeland, and partly to ensure no dissension behind his lines for the duration of the campaign. The fact that in Octavian's absence Maecenas exposed a plot against his life by Marcus Lepidus, the son of the former triumvir, indicates this was not an idle precaution.

CONFRONTATION IN GREECE

The campaign season had barely begun when Agrippa took half the fleet in a sortie against the Peloponnese and stormed Methone, eliminating Bogud in the process. It was a brilliant stroke. Antony, having deliberately established his position so far south he practically invited Octavian to enter the Balkans via Epirus, cannot have anticipated the first assault would fall on his southern flank. Detaching enough ships to harass Antony's transports as they lumbered out of the Aegean, Agrippa took the bulk of his squadron north to menace Antony's other outlying garrisons, drawing off the units that should have been patrolling Corcyra and the direct invasion route to the north. Antony had been placed on the back foot right from the outset, and the initiative would remain with Octavian for the balance of the war.

Under cover of this diversion, Octavian successfully landed his army on the coast of Epirus at Panormus (Palermo). He found Corcyra abandoned, his rival effectively surrendering to him the easy passage between the island and the mainland and securing his flank and rear as he approached the Gulf of Ambracia.

The first intelligence Antony received on Octavian's movements was word from his scouts that the enemy held Toryne (Parga), and by the time this information arrived in Patrae, Octavian had already advanced to Glycys Limen (Fanari). Reacting immediately, Antony was able to scramble the forces he had immediately available to the Gulf of Ambracia just ahead of his rival.

Octavian offered battle at sea the following day. Antony was in no position to accept this invitation. Not only had he arrived with insufficient troops to man his vessels, he found the fleet itself in a deplorable condition; fully one-third of the crews had been lost over the winter to malnutrition, disease, and desertion.

Aware that if Octavian successfully forced the entrance to the gulf he might lose the fleet, and hence the war, by default, Antony resorted to a dangerous bluff. While the oars of each ship were mounted as if waiting to be put in motion, he armed all the rowers and stationed them on the decks, the vessels being drawn up to face the enemy on either side of the entrance to the gulf, as though they were fully manned and ready for an engagement. Octavian, unwilling to run the gauntlet of fire from the towers on land while engaging with Antony's fleet in the narrows of the strait, retired.

By the end of May the confrontation had settled down to a wary stand-off. Much of the strategic direction of the ensuing campaign would be dictated by the vulnerabilities conferred on both of the contesting triumvirs by the site of their respective camps. Antony inherited and expanded the naval base established the previous year on the southern peninsula enclosing the gulf, approximately three kilometres from the temple of Apollo on the promontory of Actium. Octavian withdrew to the heights of Mikalitzi on the northern headland, extending the walls of his camp to shelter his fleet drawn up in the Bay of Comarus. The location offered commanding views of the gulf, enclosed by the mountains of the Acarnanian range to the south and Pindus range to the east. Stretching to the south-west lay the island of Leucas, the 'White Promontory,' named after its limestone cliffs (from which the poet Sappho allegedly leapt to her death) that plunge into the Ionian Sea on its western side. Separated from the mainland only by shallow lagoons, it prevented a quick turn to the south by Antony's fleet. This position inverted the advantages enjoyed by Antony's ships within the gulf; backing onto the Ionian Sea, it accorded less shelter from the elements, but Octavian's vessels were free to roam at will, while Antony's could not make for open water without offering battle.

The disadvantage of his position was that a single summer storm of sufficient magnitude to annihilate his fleet would leave Octavian stranded, with the uncomfortable options of either remaining on the coast and being pinned between Antony's army and navy, or retreating inland, giving Antony the choice of pursuit in order to seek a decisive battle or crossing unhindered to Italy.

It was clearly in Octavian's interests to force an engagement at sea sooner rather than later. The problem was that Antony was not in a position to answer the challenge even if he had failed to discern the motives behind it. Having already been depleted by its commitments to the outposts on the surrounding islands, the naval force available inside the gulf continued to erode, both in terms of numbers and fighting quality, to the point where Antony would have struggled to man and outfit as many as 300 ships, barely three-quarters of those available to his rival.

Antony, conversely, confident of his superior qualities as a general, sought to deliver the knockout blow on land. He believed the key to provoking Octavian into offering battle was a second blind spot in the location of his camp. While Octavian was the beneficiary of a salubrious climate and a commanding view from his vantage point on the heights, he did not have access to a secure source of water, being dependent on either the River Louros to the north or the two good springs in the plain to the south.

Once Antony's legions, responding to his summons from their outposts throughout the Balkans, were concentrated, he was at last in a position to

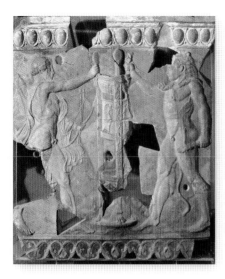

wrest the initiative back from Octavian. Crossing the strait, he established an advance camp in the plain four kilometres south of Octavian's position. Octavian responded by detaching units into Greece and Macedonia with the intention of drawing Antony off in either direction. Ignoring these feints, Antony initiated the second phase of his operative plan, ordering his cavalry and a supporting force of infantry around the inner shore of the gulf to take up a holding position north of Mikalitzi in the valley of the Louros. The intent – to cut off Octavian's water supply on both fronts and force him either to fight or withdraw – was strategically sound. But the perimeter his holding force had to maintain was over eight kilometres long and could not be effectively secured.

Whatever momentum Antony had generated in his favour was swiftly dissipated by a series of stinging setbacks. Offshore, Agrippa stormed Leucas, destroying Antony's outlying squadron there under his legate Quintus Nasidius, and seized Cape Dukato, the southern promontory of the island, thereby proffering Octavian a superior anchorage and a second depot to land supplies, while intensifying the blockade against Antony. Agrippa followed up this success by evicting the garrison at Patrae and taking possession of Antony's winter headquarters there.

The ubiquitous Agrippa ensured the noose tightened with each successive day, neutralizing even the rare local successes of the enemy. When, under cover of fog, Sosius with a detachment of Antony's fleet succeeded in exiting the strait and routing one of Octavian's naval commanders, Lucius Arruntius, on station opposite, he was intercepted by Agrippa while in pursuit and was defeated in turn.

Meanwhile, the reality that his lines were overstretched was made brutally apparent to Antony when Taurus and the renegade Titius attacked and routed his cavalry posted in the valley of the Louros, in the process inducing the defection of Philadelphus, king of Paphlagonia. The desertion of Antony's dynastic clients, who sensed the tide of war shifting in favour of Octavian, became endemic, prominent instances including Rhoemetacles of Thrace, who succeeded in attaining Octavian's camp, and Iamblichus of Emesa, whom Antony had executed before he could do likewise. The demoralizing impact of their evident lack of faith in his prospects, over and above the material accrual of strength to Octavian, contributed to a downward spiral of spirit and faith in Antony's cause. In a last bid to retrieve the situation, towards the end of August, Antony himself led a second flanking movement against Octavian's camp in person. In his absence, Amyntas went over to Octavian, taking with him his 2,000 Galatian cavalry. Antony recognized this setback as decisive and withdrew to his original camp on the southern shore.

Antony's situation was becoming desperate. Rations were short; with ever fewer of his cargo ships succeeding in running the gauntlet of Agrippa's galleys offshore, Antony was almost totally reliant on the supplies transhipped from the Aegean and trickling over the Acarnanian Mountains. With Sparta already in revolt, and Methone and Patrae now in the hands of the enemy, Antony's position in the Peloponnese was crumbling. Smouldering resentment at the impressments of local communities into the Antonian war machine (the grandfather of the historian Plutarch, for example, along with the rest of the population of Chaeronea was forced under the lash to haul requisitioned grain to Antony's agents at the nearby harbour of Anticyra) threatened to erupt throughout the rest of Greece.

Underlying every problem Antony had encountered to date was the physical environment of his camp. He had pitched his tents on marshy soil surrounded by the occasional brackish, stagnant pond. There was no running water, and the sluggish tides of the Mediterranean cannot have been enough to scour away the refuse of the more than 100,000 soldiers, sailors, and camp followers concentrated there. Conditions had been bad enough over winter; as spring turned to summer and the stalemate dragged on, Antony's army was ravaged by malaria and dysentery, which only further contributed to the steady stream of defections, despite increasingly savage examples being made of those who attempted, or considered, doing so. The loss felt most deeply by Antony was that of Ahenobarbus; grievously ill, and doubtless heartsick over the ruin of a noble Roman by the hated Egyptian queen (whom, alone of Antony's party, he had refused to acknowledge save by name), he transferred his allegiance to Octavian just before dying.

Clearly, Antony could not retain his current position; if he attempted to go into winter quarters at Actium, there would be nothing left of his army by spring. He had to break out; the question facing his council of war, itself riven by intramural hostility and sapped by increasingly self-interested disloyalty, was how, and to where?

THE BATTLE OF ACTIUM

The disposition of the forces of Antony and Octavian in the lead up to the battle of Actium. The wild card of the campaign was the weather; the strategic superiority established by Agrippa would have been inverted had a storm of sufficient magnitude disabled his fleet. (From *The Architect of the Roman Empire*, by T. Rice Holmes,1928)

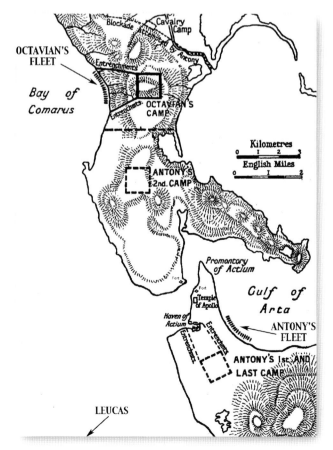

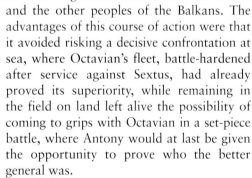

Antony convened his council of war to consider his options and arrive at a consensus. The choice narrowed down to two possible courses of action, both problematic. He could pull back by land with his entire force into Macedonia, but this would mean abandoning his fleet. Conversely, he had too few ships to embark all of his men, so even if he succeeded in breaking out by sea the bulk of the army would be left behind to fend for itself.

Canidius, who commanded the legions, made the case for the first option. He argued that Cleopatra should seek to run the blockade with her squadron and the treasury in a bid to reach Egypt while Antony should lead the army into the interior, recruiting in Greece and seeking allies from the tribes of Thrace and the other peoples of the Balkans. The advantages of this course of action were that it avoided risking a decisive confrontation at sea, where Octavian's fleet, battle-hardened after service against Sextus, had already proved its superiority, while remaining in the field on land left alive the possibility of coming to grips with Octavian in a set-piece battle, where Antony would at last be given the opportunity to prove who the better general was.

Cleopatra made the opposite case. Taking an already straitened and demoralized army up through the passes of the Pindus with the enemy at its heels risked replicating the disastrous Athenian retreat from Syracuse in similar circumstances. Even if the army did reach Macedonia it would be trapped in a Balkan cul-de-sac; Antony, having conceded total control of the sea by frittering away the immense fleet with which he had started the campaign, would not be able to force the Hellespont and attain Asia. Octavian, meanwhile, would be free to dismember the Antonian settlement of the east, or strike unhindered at Egypt itself. Saving the best part of the fleet, with the best part of the army on board, would obviate this scenario. The legions

The view from the memorial on Mikalitzi, built over the site of Octavian's camp, looking south-west towards the Ionian Sea where the battle was fought.

left behind might save themselves, and even if they didn't, those that made good their escape, supported by the 11 committed elsewhere, would form the nucleus of a new army that could be drilled over the coming winter and be ready to take the field the following spring. If nothing else, Antony and Cleopatra still had one trump card to play; while they retained the treasure of the Ptolemies they had cash reserves to keep the war going indefinitely. Octavian did not. Doubtless, Cleopatra did not raise this point before the council, but she may have privately intimated to Antony that the surrender of those legions he left behind might actually work in his favour. Octavian would be obligated to provide for their welfare, further increasing the strain on his political position. The unsatisfied claims to land and bonuses of tens of thousands of demobilized veterans kept Italy seething with tension, and Octavian had tapped out every available source of the capital he needed to keep an army and navy in the field. His financial resources and logistical capacity would be stretched, perhaps beyond breaking point, in following up on driving Antony out of Greece by having to start the next campaign season deep in Asia or Africa. Octavian's momentary ascendancy, in other words, rested on shaky foundations. So long as they kept their nerve, Antony and Cleopatra might yet emerge triumphant.

According to Orosius, when Antony, upon arriving at Actium, had found that almost a third of his rowers had died over the winter, he responded 'Let only the oars be saved, for there will be no lack of rowers, as long as Greece has men.' But the best efforts of Antony's press-gangs had failed to keep pace with the attrition rate over the summer, and the available crews were underfed, undertrained and undermotivated, hardly the best material for fight or flight.

Antony's response was to burn his excess ships, primarily the smaller warships and most of the transports. If they couldn't come with him, there was no point leaving them as gifts for Octavian. Antony was left with 230 seaworthy vessels to contest with Octavian's fleet, more than 400 strong.

His preparations complete, on the morning of 29 August, Antony embarked 20,000 legionaries, probably ten depleted legions, and 2,000 archers. The decision to confront Octavian at sea, squandering decades of hard-won experience campaigning on land in all conditions and every terrain, baffled Antony's veterans, one of whom insisted to his face:

> What have our wounds and swords done to displease you, that you should give your confidence to rotten timbers? Let Egyptians and Phoenicians contend at sea, give us the land, where we know well how to die upon the spot or gain the victory.

The view from the campsite memorial, looking south-east towards the Gulf of Ambracia. The site of Antony's camp and the bay along which his ships were moored can clearly be discerned from this distance, according Octavian a significant tactical advantage.

Antony's silence was far from reassuring. His order to embark with the sails onboard only generated more anxiety about his objectives. Antony sought to allay these concerns by explaining it was his intent to consummate victory through the pursuit and annihilation of a beaten foe: 'we must not' he maintained, 'let one enemy escape.' The falsehood of this assertion had already been established the previous evening when, under cover of night, Antony had smuggled the campaign treasury on board with Cleopatra's squadron.

Ironically, while his own camp was seething with rumour and conjecture about Antony's true intentions, Octavian radiated serene confidence in preparing his countermeasures. Not only were all of Antony's movements clearly visible from the heights of Mikalitzi, his entire plan of operation had been divulged by the last-minute defection of Dellius, who went over from Antony to Octavian, just as he had previously deserted Dolabella for Cassius and Cassius for Antony.

In the event, on 29 August and over the three following days stormy weather kept both sides cooling their heels on shore. The rough conditions, hardly conducive to a naval engagement, might otherwise have facilitated Antony's escape, but the wind consistently blew onshore from the west, making it impossible for him to round Leucas once he exited the gulf. The only action took place on 30 August, when Antony launched a diversionary assault on Octavian's camp with a few cohorts to emphasize his commitment to the war effort.

THE FLEETS EMBARK

On 2 September the skies finally cleared. Octavian embarked eight legions and five praetorian cohorts, approximately 40,000 men. He thus committed twice as many men to the battle as Antony, but dispersed across a larger number of vessels, creating an average of roughly 90 combat effectives per ship in his fleet to 110–120 per ship for Antony.

The command of the right wing of Octavian's fleet was entrusted to Marcus Lurius (the prefect of Sardinia who had been expelled by Menas on the orders of Sextus in 40 BC), the centre to Lucius Arruntius (who had sought refuge with Sextus after being proscribed in 43 BC), while Agrippa had personal command of the left wing in addition to overall command of the fleet. Such was his authority he was able to overrule Octavian's initial strategy of allowing Antony

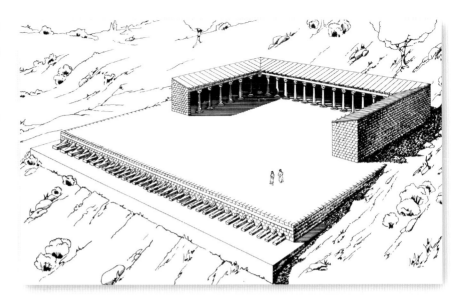

egress from the gulf unopposed, counting on the superior speed of his galleys to close on the enemy and take them from the rear. Agrippa demurred, pointing out that, since the decks of Octavian's vessels had been cleared for action, if allowed to run for open water Antony's ships would hoist sail and make good their escape. Deferring to his colleague's judgement, Octavian took up station behind his right wing on board a liburnian, stationing key subordinates in auxiliary boats to serve as couriers, dispatching his orders where necessary and reporting back to him on conditions throughout the fleet. Then he waited for the enemy to sail out.

Antony's fleet was divided into three squadrons of roughly 60 ships apiece, with another 60 in reserve under Cleopatra behind the centre. In addition to the best of his fighting men, Antony placed all his most prominent non-combatants on board, not because he felt they had anything to contribute in battle, but quite conversely to prevent them from deserting or fomenting mutiny in his absence.

Antony's sole hope for the decisive victory that would enable him to get his fleet intact out of the strategic cul-de-sac into which he had been lured was to fight as close inshore as possible to prevent Octavian from outflanking his line at either, or both, ends and taking his fleet in its rear before it could get under sail and make good its escape. In addition, the more confined the space of the battle area, the tighter the formation Antony could adopt, deterring Octavian from exploiting his numerical advantage by penetrating Antony's line and swarming individual capital ships in coordinated assaults. In a small boat Antony therefore went from one ship to the next, encouraging their crews, and personally re-emphasizing to his captains that upon clearing the gulf they were to draw up in tight formation and receive the enemy lying still, as if they were at anchor.

He then took station in his flagship, probably a class '10', on his right flank, which was commanded by Gellius Publicola, a Republican turncoat and consul for 36 BC. The left flank was commanded by Gaius Sosius. The centre was commanded by Marcus Insteius and Marcus Octavius. The career of the latter, which embodies the tangled skein of motivations that informed those fighting the civil wars of the terminal Republic, indicates that even at this stage Antony retained the loyalty of substantial military talent. A veteran

The campsite memorial today. The podium along which the rams harvested from Antony and Cleopatra's warships were displayed has collapsed along its eastern side but the sockets into which the rams were inserted are still largely intact along its western length.

of Pompey's war with Caesar, he and Scribonius Libo had joint charge of the Liburnian and Achaean fleets, defeating Dolabella on the Illyrian coast and forcing the surrender of Antony's brother Gaius. After Pharsalus, Octavius, with a considerable force still under his command, made a stand in Illyricum, where he defeated Gabinius, who was bringing reinforcements to Caesar. He was ultimately forced to fly to Africa, where he shared in the ruin of the optimates' cause at Thapsus in 46 BC.

Both armies, Canidius commanding for Antony, Taurus for Octavian, were drawn up in order along the shore on their respective promontories, silent witnesses to Antony's fleet as it exited the gulf for the last time. Drawing up on a north–south axis 'in dense array' according to Dio, Antony's ships did not seek battle but rather held station in the tightest possible formation. Plutarch remarks that Octavian could not help but admire the discipline of the enemy lying perfectly still in the straits, 'in all appearance as if they had been at anchor'. Since neither side was willing to concede the advantage to the other by closing to engage on disadvantageous terms, the stand-off continued all morning, both fleets remaining at the opposite extremities of an aquatic no man's land approximately 1.5 km wide.

The subsequent course of the encounter is indicative of the extent to which battle at sea occurs within a three-dimensional framework, as opposed to the two-dimensional nature of warfare on land. Any possibility of his achieving a decisive victory having evaporated, Antony's tactical alternatives were now dictated by the strategic considerations of topography and climate.

As both sides had learned over their months of confinement in the region, the late morning calm outside the Gulf of Ambracia does not survive into the afternoon. Around midday an offshore breeze (Virgil labels this 'the wind called Iapyx') begins to pick up. By two or three o'clock this strengthens to a brisk force 3 to 4 and, crucially, shifts from a westerly to a west-north-west direction.

With Agrippa refusing to take the bait and engage inshore, Antony's sole option was now to get as much of the fleet as possible as far out to sea as possible for it to take advantage of the wind and make good its escape by sail. The key geographic factor was the forbidding mass of Leucas, which forces any vessel bound south from the Gulf of Ambracia to set a course almost due south-west. The key technological restraint was the reality that the

A GUN CREW OPERATING A BALLISTA ON BOARD ONE OF OCTAVIAN'S GALLEYS DURING THE BATTLE OF ACTIUM (pp. 66–67)

Service onboard a galley was no soft option for those engaged in naval warfare during the classical period. No other form of combat throughout the era was so impersonal.

The galley was a finely tuned instrument of war with little margin for error in tactical manoeuvre. Ideally, the weight of every individual onboard would be integrated with that of the vessel, fully concentrating all available mass at the point of attack by its primary armament, the ram (1).

Accordingly, it was vital to minimize anything that might destabilize the vessel in order to maximize how responsive it was to the demands of the helmsman. That was easy enough below decks, where the fully enclosed oarsmen (2) of the larger galleys inhabited an isolated and anonymous world, their only stimulus the commands of the *hortatory* and the music of the piper.

Above decks it was a different story. The constraints of the galley template restricted the height relative to beam of the vessel. Simply put, the more weight on deck, the more top-heavy and hence less stable she was. The demand for ever-greater firepower and elevation meant the galleys of the late classical period were constantly pushing the envelope in terms of balancing complement and capacity vs. seaworthiness and tactical performance.

This meant the marines on both sides who went into battle at Actium had to exhibit qualities of discipline at least equal to their counterparts on land. The decks would be crowded with fighting men and stocks of missile weapons. In order to prevent the shifting weight of so many men causing the vessel to list by even a few critical degrees they were required to remain fixed to their stations, even under enemy fire, until the opportunity arose to board an enemy vessel, or they were required to repel boarders (3).

The evolution of the galley from trireme to class '10' or even higher allowed for a more stable gun platform and the incorporation of heavy ballista as missile weapons (4). These functioned strictly as the vessel's secondary armament. There were never artillery duels between galleys in the sense of one vessel seeking to immobilize or sink another solely through missile fire. The ballista was equipped to fire two forms of projectile, bolts and stones, both in an anti-personnel role, although the latter could cause considerable disruption to the rhythm of a galley's oars if plunging fire penetrated the deck and impacted among the cramped rowers below.

The wider beam of the higher classes of galley enabled the incorporation of collapsible towers as fighting platforms (5). The greater elevation of the ballista allowed for longer-range fire against distant targets and the advantage of the high ground during close-quarters action. Increased elevation, however, meant increased exposure to enemy counter-fire; even a glancing blow from a stone projectile capable of causing structural damage to a ship would be fatal to anyone caught in its path (6).

square-rigged ships of the period could not sail effectively against the wind. The best they could manage was slightly less than a right angle – in nautical terms, seven points off the wind, eight being the right angle. Simply put, the farther out to sea a ship started, the more the wind blew from astern, and the further off the wind the course lay. Antony's course from his inshore position would have been exactly seven points off the wind, the bare minimum required to clear Leucas. But the closer a ship sails to the wind, the slower her speed, and the fleet would have been crawling along at roughly two knots as it filed past the cliffs, not enough to guarantee outdistancing Octavian's energized oarsmen in pursuit. But for every kilometre he could make to seaward, the angle between the direction of the wind and the western tip of Leucas increased by half a point. Antony's tactical requirements therefore now completely inverted; from desiring battle as close inshore as possible, he now needed to engage as far out to sea as he could.

BATTLE IS JOINED

It was for this reason that as the early-afternoon breeze picked up Antony ordered his fleet to move forward. The advance was led by Sosius on his left wing which, as it lay closest inshore and furthest south, had the greatest distance to cover to get far enough seaward for its sails to be effective.

Antony may have deliberately concentrated his most powerful ships at either end of his line, deliberately thinning out his centre to draw the enemy towards the flanks, thereby enabling Cleopatra to break out by punching right through the heart of the enemy fleet. Having provided cover for Cleopatra's escape, Antony's fighting ships would then be free to disengage. Antony's strategy therefore effectively amounted to using his front-line combat vessels to lure Octavian into a total commitment of the forces under his command and keeping his eyes off the true prize, Cleopatra's squadron and the treasure secreted below decks. Offering battle was therefore integral to the success of this strategy, but it was a battle Antony knew he could not win.

Ironically, both sides now shared a common interest in Antony getting as far out to sea as possible, Antony to make good his escape, Octavian to more effectively deploy his numerical superiority and the edge his individual captains maintained in seamanship. Accordingly, as Antony's ships bore down on him, Agrippa ordered his fleet to back-water and reverse away from

OCTAVIAN'S FORCES
1 Agrippa
2 Arruntius
3 Lurius
4 Octavian

MARK ANTONY'S FORCES
A Publicola
B Octavius and Insteius
C Sosius
D Cleopatra
E Antony

xxxx
OCTAVIAN

TO SITE O
OCTAVIAN'S C

TO BAY OF COMARUS

A

1

5

6

6

N

TO LEUCAS

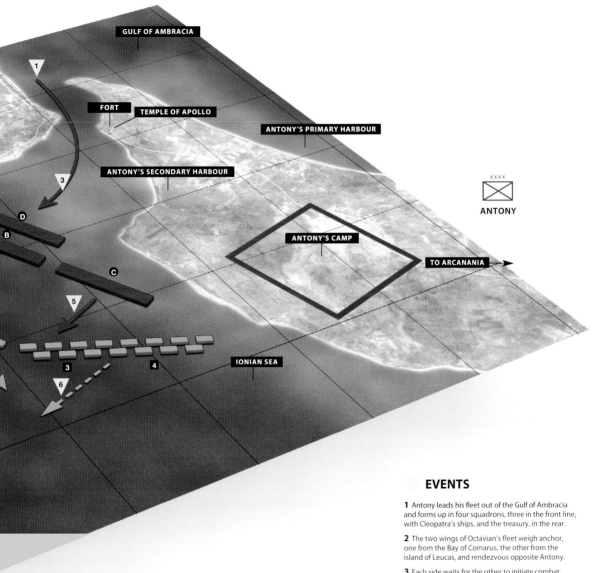

EVENTS

1 Antony leads his fleet out of the Gulf of Ambracia and forms up in four squadrons, three in the front line, with Cleopatra's ships, and the treasury, in the rear.

2 The two wings of Octavian's fleet weigh anchor, one from the Bay of Comarus, the other from the island of Leucas, and rendezvous opposite Antony.

3 Each side waits for the other to initiate combat. Antony hopes Octavian will come inshore to engage, enabling him to protect his flanks.

4 Agrippa intends to hold station until Antony advances into deep water, enabling him to exploit his numerical advantage by turning the enemy's flanks. He doubles his line to take the initial impetus out of Antony's vessels when the fleets engage.

5 Around midday Antony abandons any hope of securing a decisive victory inshore. He orders his fleet to advance, hoping to take advantage of the strengthening offshore breeze to get as many of his ships as possible away under sail.

6 Agrippa orders all three squadrons to back-water and draw Antony further away from the entrance to the gulf, intending to cut off his line of retreat in the process of encircling and annihilating his fleet.

THE MORNING OF 2 SEPTEMBER, 31 BC

Mark Antony leads his and Cleopatra's warships from the Gulf of Ambracia out into the Ionian Sea. There they clash with Octavian's fleet, which is attempting to block Antony's exit.

Ram sockets, the campsite memorial. Some of the heavier Roman galleys were built with rams well above the waterline, the intent being not to swamp the enemy, but rather to deliberately lock the two vessels together and enable boarding.

the approaching enemy. Only when Agrippa was satisfied he had created the space he needed to neutralize the advantage accorded by Antony's heavier vessels in confined waters did he give orders to reverse the tactical withdrawal and press forward. As battle was joined, Antony had already achieved half of his tactical objectives. From his new position, the course to clear Leucas bore six-and-a-half points south of west. Flight under sail would now be possible the moment the breeze reached peak intensity. The outcome of the battle therefore hinged on whether his galleys could keep the enemy at bay until that moment arrived.

Agrippa's primary concern was to ensure the initial impetus of the big Antonian ships was checked at first contact. His best option for doing so was to double his line, deploying a second row of ships to cover the intervals in his front rank. Having successfully blunted Antony's momentum, Agrippa sought to capitalize by attempting to work around Antony's right. Publicola countered by extending his line to the north.

Battle was now joined. The classic accounts are short on tactical details but vivid in depicting close-quarters combat at sea. Octavian's ships would have sought to avoid a head-on clash with Antony's heavier galleys, instead seeking to disable enemy vessels by the use of *diekplous* and *anastrophe* tactics. Agrippa must have stressed to his captains the importance of swarming enemy vessels in a coordinated fashion, isolating and immobilizing the big ships, leaving them dead in the water to be either reduced or taken at length. Accordingly, 'the engagement resembled a land fight, or, to speak yet more properly, the attack and defence of a fortified place; for there were always three or four vessels of [Octavian's] about one of Antony's, pressing them with spears, javelins, poles, and several inventions of fire, which they flung among them, Antony's men using ballistae also, to pour down missiles from wooden towers.'

Dio emphasizes the hit-and-run nature of the tactics employed by Octavian's galleys. In his account, the movements of Octavian's vessels corresponded to those of cavalry, using their superior speed to alternately charge and retreat:

Since they dreaded the long-range missiles of the enemy no less than their fighting at close-quarters, they wasted no time either in the approach or in the encounter, but running up suddenly so as to reach their object before the enemy's archers could get in their work, they would inflict injuries or else cause just enough disturbance to escape being held, and then would retire out of range.

Because a '6' could not long survive exposure to a '10' before its decks were swept clean by superior firepower, teamwork was critical to this risky cycle of commitment and withdrawal. Ideally, two or three ships would simultaneously approach one of Antony's, some doing all the damage they could while the others took the brunt of the return fire. Antony's crews, by contrast, aimed to hit the approaching ships with dense showers of stones and arrows, and, once they were within range, to snag them with grapnels.

In taking the classic accounts at face value the conflict at Actium can be interpreted as a prototype of the form naval warfare would assume for the next 1,800 years. The classic period of the galley, the contest decided by skill with oar and ram, was over; the new era was defined by dexterous manoeuvre of the fleet into the best possible conditions for the hand-to-hand slugfest that was to follow. In those terms, the tactical dispositions and nature of the conflict at Actium would not have appeared foreign to veterans of Sluys (1340), Lepanto (1571), or even Trafalgar (1815).

However, it is important to reflect on the fact that the classic accounts all derived from, and subsequently played a role in amplifying, Augustan propaganda. Octavian shaped interpretation of the battle to conform with the geopolitical construct he had established over the past decade wherein he embodied the Roman order as defined against the alien and hostile east. Paterculus reiterated this tradition when he described Octavian and Antony as having 'led out their fleets and fought, the one for the safety, the other for the ruin, of the world.'

In order to stress the heroic, above and beyond the inherently righteous, nature of Octavian's cause, it was necessary to portray him as the underdog struggling to preserve the Roman way of life against overwhelming enemy force. Because there was no way to disguise the reality that Antony was in fact heavily outnumbered by the time he offered battle, great emphasis was placed on the disparity between the size of the ships relative to each fleet. Each classic account makes a particular reference to the imposing bulk of the vessels, ranging in class up to the '10', under Antony's command, which achieve

LEFT
Looking north towards Octavian's campsite on Mikalitzi from the walls of Nikopolis, the sanctuary of Apollo visible in the middle distance. Antony constructed his forward camp on this spot in a bid to cut off Octavian's access to the springs in the vicinity and pressure him into offering battle.

RIGHT
Looking north along the Bay of Comarus. Until Agrippa succeeded in seizing Leucas, offering an alternate harbour for at least some of his ships, Octavian's entire fleet was beached here, protected from land by walls extending from his camp on Mikalitzi to the shore, and, to a limited extent, from the weather by a mole built out into the water.

CLEOPATRA'S SQUADRON BREAKS OUT OF THE MÊLÉE AT ACTIUM (pp. 74–75)

The climax at Actium occurred at mid-afternoon, when the offshore breeze had strengthened to the point where Cleopatra's reserve squadron could hoist sail and make good its escape, getting the Ptolemaic queen and her treasury clear of Octavian's blockade.

Antony's heavily outnumbered frontline squadrons have been struggling for over two hours to hold Octavian's ships at bay. With the last of Cleopatra's vessels now receding over the horizon (1) those of Antony's ships that are still capable of doing so are finally free to disengage and seek their own way out of the mêlée. In order to lighten the load their crews are frantically ditching everything they can spare overboard, including the now superfluous fighting towers (2).

After going toe-to-toe with Octavian's battle-hardened veteran crews, many of whom served under Agrippa at Mylae and Naulochus prior to the Actium campaign, the order to break out has come too late for most of Antony's ships. The galley in the left foreground is not going anywhere (3). Enemy incendiaries have set her sails ablaze. She cannot escape by rowing clear because her oars have been sheared off on her starboard side.

Even if she still had propulsion, the vulnerable steering oars in her stern have also been lost to enemy action, making navigation impossible. Immobilized, she can do little more than wait until she attracts the attention of Octavian's galleys, now swarming through the gaps as Antony's lines disintegrate.

One of Antony's superships, a '10' has already been isolated in this fashion (4). An enemy '6' is exchanging broadsides to port (5), giving cover for another '6' approaching to ram from astern starboard (6).

The gathering clouds overhead herald the doom of another of Antony's galleys (7). As the wind picked up in the late afternoon the water began to get choppy, then rough. This was more stress than the vessel in the foreground could take. Rammed repeatedly below the waterline over the course of the battle she has swamped, listing heavily to port. Already destabilized, the bow wave from another galley passing nearby is enough to tip her over completely on her side. If they are lucky, the remnant of the marines onboard still desperately clinging to her prow may be picked up by one of the longboats (*scaphae*) scuttling about the combat zone in a search-and-rescue role (8).

monstrous proportions in the retelling. Florus describes Antony's ships as 'rising high out of the water with towers and platforms so as to resemble fortresses or cities.' The largest class of Octavian's vessels, by contrast, was the '6'. Because of this disparity, Dio maintains an eyewitness might have compared the spectacle of Octavian's galleys swarming around those of Antony to 'walled towns or else islands, many in number and close together, being besieged from the sea'.

A number of caveats must be assigned to these accounts. Firstly, the authors overemphasize the actual distinction in size between the vessels of the rival fleets. Advances in nautical engineering and the evolution in strategic functionality notwithstanding, naval warfare throughout the classical period could not escape the technical limitations inherent in the galley template. It is surprising to consider just how marginal in terms of freeboard the advantage conferred by the '10' actually was. Orosius lets this cat out of the bag when he remarks that while Antony's ships were inferior in number, 'they excelled in size, for in height they were ten feet above the sea.' While this height advantage would be extended by the towers erected fore and aft, which, because of the broader beam of the '10' would be more massive than those supported by the '6', it is simply inaccurate to conceive of the '10' as looming, Olympus-like, over the battle.

Secondly, the sources all stress Octavian was able to turn the unwieldy mass of Antony's fleet to his advantage. Paterculus describes Antony's capital ships as being 'formidable in appearance only.' Florus makes the point that while Antony's ships 'made the sea groan and the wind labour as they moved along,' ultimately their very bulk 'was fatal to them,' as they were 'clumsy and in every respect unwieldy.' Plutarch agrees, noting of Antony's 'huge vessels' that 'their size and their want of men made them slow to move and difficult to manage.' In this manner, the valour and fighting quality of the west trumps the extravagance and folly of the east, thereby drawing parallels between Rome and Greece, Cleopatra and Persia, Antony and Xerxes, Octavian and Themistocles, in maintaining a tradition dating back to Salamis nearly four-and-a-half centuries earlier.

Lastly, only briefly touched on in the classic accounts but confirmed by archaeological evidence, there is the fact that not every ship under Antony's command exceeded Octavian's in size. While Octavian's fleet comprised classes '2' to '6', Antony's ranged from classes '4' to '10'. There was plenty of overlap within that spectrum. In fact, close analysis by Murray concludes Antony was able to commit no more than five of class '10', four of class '9',

five of class '8', and six of class '7' to engage Octavian. The 'siege warfare' interpretation of the battle, therefore, is a highly selective one. Most of Octavian's ships would not in fact have been tasked with swarming against isolated and lumbering behemoths. The bulk of the fighting would have taken place between vessels in the same class.

Accordingly, we are in a position to interpret the battle more accurately. Antony would have used his higher classes to anchor each squadron, hoping they would draw in enough of Octavian's vessels to cut down the odds against his class '5' and '6' ships and give them the freedom of manoeuvre they needed to respond to Octavian's bid to stretch and outflank his first line. The outcome would hang on whether by this stratagem Antony could hold Octavian at bay long enough to get Cleopatra clear. From this interpretation it becomes apparent that, far from constituting the cream of the naval force under his command, the primary function of Antony's much-heralded superships by this point amounted to little more than serving as bait. Realistically, he can only have expected his smaller and lighter ships to be in a position to disengage and slip away once Cleopatra made good her escape. Because they would be heavily committed from the initial clash, and their bulk limited their speed even under sail in any case, he fully anticipated leaving his higher classes behind.

In the event, as Agrippa continued to focus on turning Antony's right flank, Publicola, determined to prevent him from circling into the rear of Antony's line, slowly wheeled his squadron from a north–south axis to an east–west one. As he did so he lost contact with the centre, which itself thinned out as the ships on both sides sought space to secure tactical advantage.

THE BREAKOUT

It was roughly two hours after battle commenced, just as the breeze was reaching its peak intensity, when Cleopatra made her move. Dio maintains Cleopatra fled because she lost her nerve; 'true to her nature as a woman and an Egyptian', she gave the signal for her squadron, which had not yet been engaged, to hoist sail and break out through the now disordered centre of Octavian's line. In reality, this venture had been prearranged. Cleopatra had in fact coolly held position until judging, accurately, that the wind had picked up sufficiently to get her clear under sail.

Antony, observing Cleopatra's flight, transferred his flag to a '5' and hastened after her. Those of his galleys that were not immobilized or too closely

engaged with the enemy in turn raised their sails and sought gaps in Octavian's line through which to break out. As they departed they dumped their towers, their reinforced hull plating, and any other of the now superfluous accoutrements of war overboard in order to lighten their vessels and increase their speed. As anticipated, once clear of Leucas, further harassment was minimal. Eurycles led some of Octavian's liburnians in pursuit of the fleeing ships and succeeded in hauling in two of them, but otherwise the fugitives, comprising Cleopatra's squadron and the handful of other vessels that had managed to extricate themselves from the mêlée, got away clean.

Octavian could now claim the victory. Determined to save as many as possible of Antony's ships, and their crews, that remained in the theatre for his own future use, he raced from vessel to vessel, shouting and pointing out to those on board that Antony had fled, and asking them for whom, and with whom, they were still fighting.

But Octavian's exhortations, the hopelessness of their situation, and even the flight of their commander, could not induce Antony's loyalists to seek terms. When Octavian's galleys closed to board them, expecting to take easy prizes, their crews pushed their assailants back with boathooks, cut them down with axes, and bombarded them with stones and other missiles.

TOP LEFT
View from Fort Pantokrator, looking west out into the Ionian Sea. Of all the legions Antony abandoned at Actium, the garrison he stationed here would have had the final view of their erstwhile commander, making off after Cleopatra under sail from right to left across the horizon.

TOP RIGHT
Antony's fleet was beached the length of this bay stretching along the interior of the Gulf of Ambracia.

BOTTOM
To this day, stagnant water still collects in pools across the low-lying site of Antony's camp, the perfect breeding ground for disease-bearing mosquitoes.

The castle of Christ Pantokrator, a Venetian fort inherited and expanded on in 1807 by the renegade Ottoman warlord Ali Pasha to secure the north side of the entrance to the Gulf of Ambracia. Antony's fort would have been constructed on the same site for the same purpose.

Determined to bring closure to a conflict that no longer served any purpose, Octavian's captains increasingly resorted to deploying fire as the means to stamp out the Antonian diehards. They would approach their victims from many directions simultaneously, subjecting them to a barrage of flaming ballista bolts and arrows, pots full of charcoal and pitch, and even torches fastened to javelins. If these incendiary weapons were not immediately doused or dumped overboard they would catch and ignite. Antony's vessels would have been especially vulnerable to this form of attack; after months spent under the hot summer sun, the timbers of his ships must have been bone dry, and stowing the flammable sails on deck could hardly have improved their resistance to fire. In a particularly gripping passage, Dio relates that when the crews ran out of water to combat the spreading flames they sought to smother them by piling blankets and even any corpses at hand on top of them. This temporary expedient failed when the breeze continued to pick up, igniting the smouldering mounds. In such circumstances, some of the crew would hew away or scatter the timbers, the more enterprising individuals hurling them against their opponents. Others would now more than ever make use of their grappling-irons and hooks in a bid to bind some hostile ship to theirs, crossing over to it, if possible, or, if not, allowing the flames to spread and forcing it to participate in their fiery demise.

At around four o'clock the weather began to deteriorate. Those of Antony's ships that remained in the theatre, by now subjected to significant structural damage from the pounding they had taken over the past four hours, were most at risk from the rising seas. Confronted with the reality that the only options available were capitulation or death by drowning, suicide, or immolation, even the most recalcitrant Antonians began to raise their oars in a gesture of surrender. Octavian, anxious to cover any contingency, remained on station in the gulf all night. But as evening fell the only vessels remaining outside his control were the blazing hulks whose flames would have punctuated the darkness until, one by one, guttering out.

Dawn would have revealed a sea and shoreline thick with the detritus of battle; the waves, as depicted by Florus, 'continually yielded up the purple and gold-bespangled spoils of the Arabians and Sabaeans and a thousand other Asiatic peoples.' Our sources on casualties conflict; Plutarch concludes that Antony lost less than 5,000 men killed; Orosius cites reports of Antony losing 12,000 dead and another 6,000 wounded, of whom 1,000 subsequently died. No figures survive to enumerate Octavian's losses.

Mapping these figures against the outcome of the battle is problematic. Do they refer specifically to the battle, or to the campaign as a whole? Can the discrepancy be reconciled by assuming Plutarch's figure refers only to Antony's fighting men, while Orosius includes his oarsmen and crews? Can we use either total to draw conclusions about the number of ships lost? And what does the silence about Octavian's casualties hide? The fact he did not immediately seek to end the war by ordering an aggressive pursuit of the fugitives suggests he was nursing a fleet too badly bruised in the course of the battle to follow up in the aftermath.

ANTONY'S DEFEAT

Nevertheless, there is no contesting the scale of Octavian's victory. Murray concludes he took as trophies the rams from 330 to 350 vessels captured throughout the course of the campaign, a figure that includes those salvaged from the hulks burned by Antony prior to the final battle. Discounting the 60 that escaped with Cleopatra, and the additional handful that also succeeded in disengaging, either during the battle or later from Antony's surviving outlying garrisons, this leaves roughly 100 unaccounted for from Antony's original armada of 500. Some of these would have been lost to Agrippa's raids and other preliminary actions, but we have no reason to doubt the toll on his fighting galleys incurred by Antony as the price of breaking free from the largely self-imposed trap at Actium was substantial. Put another way, if we set aside the 90 vessels that made good their escape – the 60 in Cleopatra's squadron and, at most, another 30 that subsequently succeeded in fighting their way out – then Antony lost a total of 140 ships taken or destroyed over the course of four hours' fighting, 60.9 per cent of his fleet.

This fact no doubt weighed heavily on Antony's mind. Taken aboard Cleopatra's flagship, he went forwards by himself, and sat alone, without a word, in the ship's prow, covering his face with both hands. He remained in this posture for three days until the refugee fleet touched at Taenarus, where Cleopatra's handmaids prevailed upon the two of them to speak together. While they were docked, stragglers continued to trickle in, bringing news of his once mighty armada being utterly destroyed, but that the army still stood firm. Antony sent messengers to Canidius to march with all speed through Macedonia into Asia. After providing for those of his friends and associates he felt would be safer going to ground in Greece, Antony set sail for Alexandria.

On the face of it, Antony's strategic situation was far from hopeless. He had managed to extricate a significant proportion of his fleet from a very difficult position, enough vessels to serve as the nucleus for the new navy a vigorous programme of shipbuilding over the winter could provide him. He had saved the treasury of Egypt. Once Canidius completed the withdrawal from Macedonia and reunited his forces with those in the east, Antony would have a substantial number of legions at his command, enough to ensure the continued loyalty of his client potentates.

Antony minted a series of coins dedicated to the individual legions under his command during the Actian War. This example recognizes the XVI Legion, depicting its eagle standard (*aquila*) flanked by two century standards (*signa*).

The XII Legion had a storied history. Raised as the *Victrix* in 57 BC by Caesar, it served with him during his Gallic and Civil wars. Reconstituted as the *Antiqua* by Lepidus in 43 BC, it served with Antony against Parthia and at Actium. Subsequently renamed *Fulminata* by Octavian it served with distinction in the east for more than four centuries.

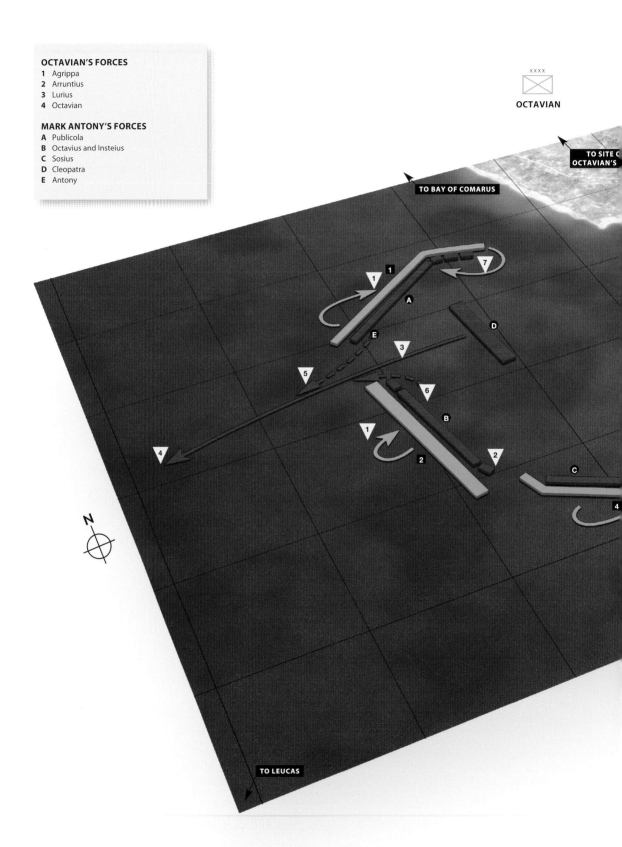

OCTAVIAN'S FORCES
1 Agrippa
2 Arruntius
3 Lurius
4 Octavian

MARK ANTONY'S FORCES
A Publicola
B Octavius and Insteius
C Sosius
D Cleopatra
E Antony

OCTAVIAN

TO SITE C
OCTAVIAN'S

TO BAY OF COMARUS

TO LEUCAS

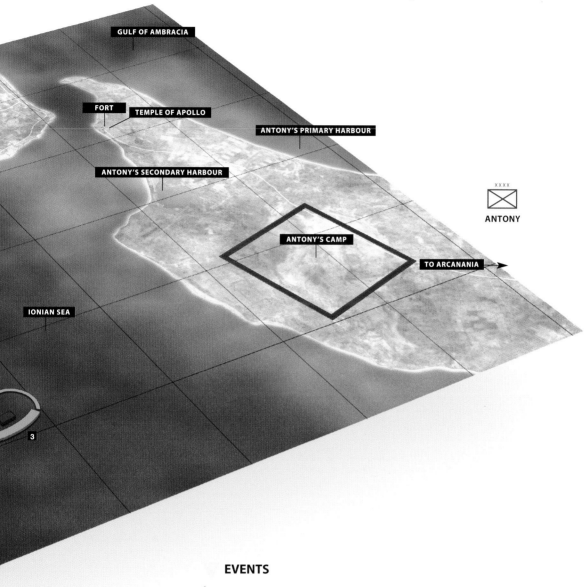

GULF OF AMBRACIA

FORT

TEMPLE OF APOLLO

ANTONY'S PRIMARY HARBOUR

ANTONY'S SECONDARY HARBOUR

xxxx
ANTONY

ANTONY'S CAMP

TO ARCANANIA

IONIAN SEA

3

EVENTS

1 Agrippa signals the fleet to reverse its tactical withdrawal and advance to engage.

2 All three of Antony's squadrons lose cohesion and contact with each other as they struggle to contain the swarms of enemy ships seeking to pass through or around their lines. Antony's super heavy ships in particular are isolated and are reduced by packs of enemy vessels.

3 As Agrippa seeks to turn Antony's right flank Publicola pivots and stretches his squadron from a north–south to an east–west axis in response. As it does so a gap opens up between these squadrons and the central sector of the combat zone.

4 At mid-afternoon, as the offshore breeze reaches its maximum strength, and approximately two hours after the onset of battle, Cleopatra's squadron hoists sail and

breaks out through the gap between Agrippa's and Arruntius's squadrons.

5 Antony transfers his flag to a lighter vessel and sets off after Cleopatra.

6 Any vessels in Antony's fleet still capable of disengaging and making good their escape now do so.

7 Agrippa is now able to outflank the remnant of Antony's fleet on what remains of both lines. Antony's ships fight on, but taken on all sides simultaneously and with no possibility of either succour or flight one by one they surrender or are destroyed.

8 Rough weather returns in the late afternoon. Octavian remains on station all night, but the first light of dawn confirms his victory is complete.

THE AFTERNOON OF 2 SEPTEMBER, 31 BC

As the wind picks up, Cleopatra's squadron manages to break through Octavian's forces. Antony also escapes, but his remaining forces are destroyed.

In fact, the war was effectively over. The most significant consequence of Antony's flight at Actium was the response of his legionaries. Plutarch relates that only a handful of the men left behind had known Antony's intent was flight, and those who were told of it at first refused to believe he had abandoned them. Some asserted the entire affair had been a ruse, and that Antony would materialize unexpectedly from some quarter and again take his accustomed place at their head.

But when Canidius broke camp and commenced the retreat, the rank and file, now forced to accept the reality of Antony's departure, simply refused to hazard another perilous march with a powerful enemy at their heels through unforgiving terrain towards an uncertain future. The veterans, who best understood the dynamics of civil war, commenced impromptu negotiations intended to secure the best possible terms in exchange for their surrender. They held out for equal treatment with the victorious army, and a guarantee those six legions most loyal to their standards be retained intact rather than being dissolved, their rank and file dispersed throughout Octavian's own legions, the fate of the others. This agreed upon, and their erstwhile commander Canidius having slipped away during the night, on 9 September, the greater part of ten legions, their light-armed and auxiliary troops, and as many as 10,000 cavalry, formally swore allegiance to Octavian.

This disaster, which set the seal on the outcome of the civil war, was not inevitable. It sprang from Antony's failure to recognize his obligations in this, the supreme crisis of his career. There was no reason for Antony to personally lead his fleet into battle at Actium. He had never previously commanded in a set-piece naval battle and had capable subordinates who could have brought Cleopatra out of the theatre, who in fact would have considered separating her from Antony the greatest blessing of fortune enjoyed by the campaign to date, possibly even the turning point of the war.

Antony's place was with the legions he left behind on shore. Had he led them away from Actium they would have followed, just as they had after the setbacks at Mutina in 43 BC and Phraaspa seven years later. This was the opportunity for Antony's best qualities to emerge, leading by example, rallying his men, personally reminding them the wheel of fortune would turn in their favour again, just as it always had before, if they would only remain loyal. Only Antony could have saved Antony's army, and in doing so revived the legend of the commander who always beat the odds to fight again another day. In choosing to break out by sea instead of fighting his way out by land, Antony not only shattered this image, but irrevocably broke the bond of comradeship he had established with men whose proudest boast had been to say they served under him.

The classic sources thus universally ascribe to the queen of Egypt the blame for Antony's downfall. Plutarch scorns his choice to display 'to all the world that he was no longer driven by the thoughts and motives of a commander or a man, or indeed by his own judgement at all, and what was once said as a jest, that the soul of a lover lives in someone else's body, he proved to be a serious truth. For, as if he had been born part of her, and must move with her wherever she went,' when he saw Cleopatra fleeing the battle he hastened to follow, abandoning those who were fighting and dying for him 'to follow her that had so well begun his ruin and would hereafter accomplish it.'

This painting by Lawrence Alma-Tadema, *Antony and Cleopatra* (1885), beautifully captures the mood on board Cleopatra's flagship during the flight from Actium.

The implications of this servility were clear to the authors of the imperial era: 'one might question whether in case of victory he would have acted according to Cleopatra's will or his own,' Paterculus notes. The inference, again upholding the Augustan tradition, is of Antony having forfeited the Roman identity Octavian championed. Had the outcome at Actium therefore been reversed, Cleopatra, not Antony, eastern, not western, civilization would have triumphed.

But, however distorted they have come down to us by a hostile historical narrative, the fact remains Antony's actions were ultimately motivated by a force that makes its perhaps unique contribution to military history during the campaign at Actium, call it what you will – fidelity, devotion, love. In this sense the sources are correct in accusing Antony of behaving irrationally. His fatally compromised judgement made for great drama but poor strategy. The fact a man could be so besotted he would throw away an army and any chance to win a war simply because he could not bear to be absent from the side of the woman he loved is what inspires our unique fascination over this last struggle to inherit the Republic. But at the end of the day, it ensured Rome's imperial destiny would be dictated by the cool genius of Octavian, not the impulsively dutiful Antony.

THE AFTERMATH

The fragility of Antony's position was made almost immediately apparent upon his return to Egypt. Temporarily detaching from Cleopatra, he sailed to Cyrenaica to link up with Pinarius Scarpus and his four legions. But Scarpus had already been alerted to the outcome at Actium. He executed Antony's heralds, and purged in like fashion any in the ranks still loyal to their erstwhile commander-in-chief. Stymied, Antony proceeded to Alexandria.

In Rome, it was the orator Cicero's son, Marcus, who had the satisfaction of reading to the Senate Octavian's dispatch announcing Antony's defeat. The younger Cicero had been among those Republican idealists who had sided with Brutus after the ides of March and served under him at Philippi. Octavian's gesture, enabling him to take some small measure of revenge for the death of his father, was further evidence of the care Octavian took to legitimize his regime by associating it with the Republican traditions of Rome. Reconciliation was the order of the day. When Octavian entered upon his fourth consulship in 30 BC his colleague was Marcus Licinius Crassus, the grandson of Caesar's colleague in the First Triumvirate; originally attached to Sextus, he had fled to Antony after Naulochus and then deserted to Octavian on the eve of Actium.

Cleopatra's gambit in having her Red Sea fleet readied to transport her treasure, and possibly her children, to the east in the event of Egypt succumbing to Octavian was foiled when King Malchus of the Nabatean Arabs, striking out of his inaccessible desert capital here at Petra, burned her ships.

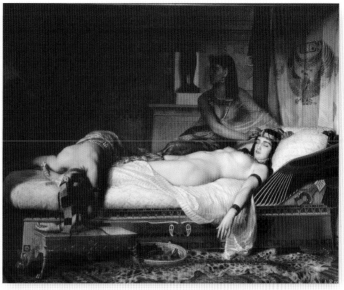

All of Greece save Corinth (which was seized by Agrippa) declared for Octavian after Actium, enabling him to cross over from Athens to Asia Minor. But, once again, the financial burden of victory threatened to undermine everything he had achieved. Already struggling to pay those veterans who had enlisted in his name, he now had to satisfy the demands of the legions he inherited from Antony. Octavian was holding court on Samos settling affairs – which included confirming on their thrones Antony's clients Amyntas, Polemo, and Archelaus, all of whom had without scruple thrown themselves on the mercy of the victor at Actium – when word arrived from Italy that the discharged veterans were near revolt.

With no option but to resolve these grievances in person, Octavian was forced to risk a winter voyage home. Suetonius adds the dramatic details of his losing ships during two violent storms en route, the spars and rigging of his own vessel being carried away and the rudder broken in pieces, before arriving at Brundisium at the end of January. He was only able to defuse the impending collapse of the social order by promising money to all and land to the veterans, using the treasure of the Ptolemies as security. Octavian was now mortgaged to the hilt; if he could not get his hands on Cleopatra's treasure the house of cards that constituted his political order would come crashing down.

After a 27-day interlude at Brundisium Octavian departed again for the east, on this occasion taking the precaution of avoiding the rough passage around the Peloponnese by hauling his ships across the isthmus of Corinth. He arrived back in Asia at the end of February, early enough in the sailing season to prevent Antony from hearing about, and taking advantage of, the domestic crises in Italy. By early spring Octavian, ready for the final reckoning with Antony and Cleopatra, initiated a two-pronged invasion of Egypt from east and west simultaneously.

Antony was meanwhile entertaining the last of his clients, Herod, in Alexandria. The king's advice was for Antony to liquidate Cleopatra and seize Egypt and its treasure for Rome, stripping Octavian of the justification for waging a foreign war and impelling him to come to terms. It was Antony's last trump card; he refused to play it. Herod promptly defected to Octavian, as did Antony's governor in Syria, Didius.

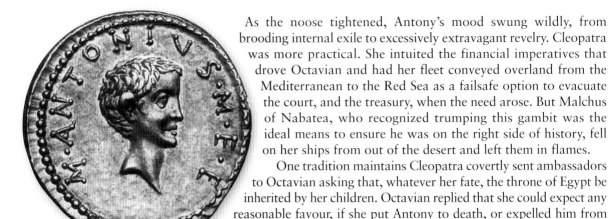

Marcus Antonius Minor, commonly refered to by his diminutive, Antyllus, was the eldest child of Mark Antony from his third wife Fulvia. His decision to quit the household of his stepmother Octavia and serve with his father sealed his fate; he was the only one of Antony's children put to death by Octavian after the annexation of Egypt. (Courtesy Wayne Sayles)

As the noose tightened, Antony's mood swung wildly, from brooding internal exile to excessively extravagant revelry. Cleopatra was more practical. She intuited the financial imperatives that drove Octavian and had her fleet conveyed overland from the Mediterranean to the Red Sea as a failsafe option to evacuate the court, and the treasury, when the need arose. But Malchus of Nabatea, who recognized trumping this gambit was the ideal means to ensure he was on the right side of history, fell on her ships from out of the desert and left them in flames.

One tradition maintains Cleopatra covertly sent ambassadors to Octavian asking that, whatever her fate, the throne of Egypt be inherited by her children. Octavian replied that she could expect any reasonable favour, if she put Antony to death, or expelled him from the country. Whatever the veracity in accounts of this exchange, Cleopatra remained, at the last, true to Antony. It was fitting, given everything he had sacrificed for her, that when the end came, she should share in his fate.

With Scarpus having gone over to Octavian, Egypt's western frontier was wide open. Incorporating the four erstwhile Antonian legions in his army, Cornelius Gallus advanced on and occupied Paraetonium (Marsa Matruh). Antony moved against Gallus with a large combined force, hoping to win back the loyalty of the men who had served under him, but his entreaties were drowned out when Gallus ordered his trumpeters to sound their instruments all together, giving no one a chance to hear a word.

Antony subsequently failed in a bid to storm the city walls and later suffered a reverse with his ships as well. Gallus took no overt measures to protect the city from the seaward side, but at night secretly stretched chains under water across the mouth of the harbour. When Antony's vessels sailed inside, the chains were drawn taut and the trap was sprung.

Antony returned to Alexandria in time to receive the news that Pelusium, the anchor of Egypt's defences in the east, had opened its gates to Octavian without resistance.

Cleopatra had ordered construction of a mausoleum, adjacent to the temple of Isis, within which she now deposited her treasure – gold, silver, emeralds, pearls, ebony, ivory, cinnamon – interspersed with a great quantity of torchwood and pitch. She was sending a clear signal of her intention to destroy the riches of her kingdom rather than let them fall into the hands of Octavian, who accordingly, Plutarch notes, even while marching on her capital, 'omitted no occasion of giving her new assurances of his good intentions.'

THE FALL OF EGYPT

By 31 July Octavian's scouts had penetrated into the suburbs of Alexandria as far as the Hippodrome. There was time for one last victory, one last manifestation of the old, impetuous Antony. He made a fierce sally, routed the enemy's cavalry, and beat them back to their lines. Returning in fine ardour to the palace, in full armour he embraced Cleopatra, kissed her, and commended to her one of his men, who had distinguished himself in the fight, to whom she presented a breastplate and helmet of gold. But that evening a discordant note of realism injected itself into the romantic façade being maintained at court when this selfsame hero took his trophies and deserted to Octavian.

Brought to bay, Antony resorted to every stratagem he could devise in a bid to narrow the odds. He shot arrows into Octavian's camp carrying leaflets promising six thousand sesterces to every deserter, but the response was derisory. He challenged Octavian to single combat, but only received a reply suggesting he consider the several other more practical alternatives to ending his life.

For Antony there was no death more honourable than in battle. At dawn on 1 August he marched his army out of Alexandria and posted them on high ground, from which he observed his fleet approach the enemy. But far from engaging, his vessels raised their oars in a gesture of surrender. Immediately upon their being received into Octavian's navy the combined squadrons established a cordon around the city. There would be no escape by sea.

No sooner had Antony witnessed this than his cavalry, too, deserted him. With their flanks stripped bare Antony's foot were routed. He fell back into the city, crying out that Cleopatra had betrayed him to the enemies he had made for her sake. She, in fear of his irrational wrath, barricaded herself in her mausoleum and sent messengers to inform Antony she was dead. Believing it, he turned his sword on himself. He succeeded only in inflicting a mortal wound rather than securing a quick death, but his botched attempt at suicide did allow him to live long enough to learn Cleopatra was still very much alive. Brought to her, he at least had the satisfaction of dying in her arms.

Having taken the city almost bloodlessly, Octavian's priority was securing the treasury, Cleopatra's last trump card. With a simple ruse he succeeded in seizing both the riches of Egypt and its queen intact.

Octavian allowed Cleopatra to bury Antony with full honours but otherwise kept her under the closest guard, a prisoner in her own gilded cage. Disposing of her was a vexatious problem; she could not be allowed to live, but executing her would be unseemly and could potentially incite a popular revolt throughout Egypt.

He hit upon the stratagem of allowing a confidant to intimate Octavian was due to depart Alexandria in three days and intended for Cleopatra and her infant children to adorn his triumph in Rome. As he had hoped, rather than be subjected to this indignity, Cleopatra arranged, in her final *coup de théâtre*, for her own suicide. At 39 years of age, for 22 of which she had reigned as queen, she was laid to rest next to Antony.

The subsequent bloodletting was light, liquidation being restricted to those for whom there was no place under the new regime. These included Antony's last loyalists, most prominently Canidius, and the last of Caesar's assassins, Turullius and Cassius of Parma.

Caesarion had been sent by his mother, with a great sum of money, into exile in India. It is one of the more fascinating what-ifs of history to construct an alternate timeline where he, the true heir of Caesar, made good his escape and established a Julio-Ptolemaic dynasty in the orient, he or one of his descendants someday sweeping out of the east, like a reverse Alexander, to seize Rome and claim his patrimony. But it wasn't to be; he was betrayed into Octavian's hands en route, and a rival Caesar was too dangerous to be allowed to live.

Antyllus, to whom Octavian's daughter Julia had been betrothed at the conference of Tarentum, sought sanctuary at a shrine Cleopatra had erected to the memory of Caesar. He was dragged from the statue, to which he was clinging, and slain. Antony's younger son by Fulvia, Iullus, was allowed to live and served Octavian loyally before being condemned to death in 2 BC when his affair with Julia was exposed.

Statue of a boy wearing the tunic, leggings, and elaborate pyramidal tiara of Armenian royalty, possibly representing Antony's son, Alexander Helios, who was confirmed in his inheritance of Armenia during the Donations of Alexandria. (The Metropolitan Museum of Art, Edith Perry Chapman Fund, 1949 [49.11.3]. Image © The Metropolitan Museum of Art)

Of Antony's children by Cleopatra, the ten-year-old twins Cleopatra Selene and Alexander Helios appeared in Octavian's triumph, alongside their six-year-old brother Ptolemy Philadelphus, all three siblings clad in chains of gold so heavy they could not walk. Selene was subsequently married off to King Juba II of Mauretania; her brothers disappear from history. Selene's son, the last Ptolemy, ruled the kingdom from AD 23 to 40 until his execution at the hands of his cousin, the emperor Caligula, one of three future emperors, including Claudius and Nero, descended from Antony's daughter Octavia.

FROM REPUBLIC TO EMPIRE

Octavian, at 35 years of age, was now undisputed master of the world. His overt imprint on the territories directly or indirectly under his domain was deliberately, and deceptively, small. He retained Antony's settlement of the east largely intact – of the bequests confirmed at the Donations of Alexandria, only Cyprus and Cyrenaica reverted to Roman provincial status. The frontier was pacified through recognition of the right of Armenia, Media and Parthia to exist outside the Roman system, at least for now.

Octavian, taking office as consul for the fifth time that year, returned to Rome in 29 BC. He celebrated three triumphs on consecutive days (13, 14, and 15 August) to commemorate his victories in Illyricum, at Actium, and in Egypt, the last being especially notable, not merely for the quantity and splendour of the spoils on display, but also for the effigy of the dead Cleopatra, lying on her couch with the asp clinging to her arm.

For those few who still cared to notice such things, it may have appeared ominous that whereas traditionally the magistrates and officials of Rome led the *triumphator* into the city, they now followed behind his chariot. But a citizen body scarred by generations of insurrection and civil war had no incentive to second guess the man who had ordered, for only the third time in Roman history, the double bronze doors at either end of the arched gate of Janus Quirinus in the Forum be closed, signifying the Republic was, at last, at peace.

This achieved, Octavian's priority was the reduction of the 60 legions under his command. The accumulated wealth of Egypt not only released so much liquidity into the Roman economy that the standard rate of interest

The Death of Dido, from the *Vergilius Vaticanus*, an illuminated manuscript dated *c.* AD 400. Aeneas, last scion of Troy, having forsaken his own desires in Carthage in pursuit of his duty, Queen Dido, unable to endure his absence, mounts her funeral pyre and falls on the sword Aeneas gave her. Virgil's message in his *Aeneid* was clear; the contrast between Aeneas, who put country above self, and Antony, who fell under the spell of his oriental queen, explicit.

dropped from twelve to four percent, it enabled the discharge of over 100,000 veterans, with full bounties paid, to settlements in the colonies in Italy or the provinces.

Octavian's unilateral proclamation ending the wars was in one way problematic, for it raised the question of the status of the Republican constitution; the legitimacy of the unprecedented authority centralized in his person, after all, was derived from the crisis brought on by Cleopatra's threat to Rome, and now that threat had passed. Octavian toyed with the idea of laying down his extraordinary powers, but, in the words of Suetonius, after concluding that it would be both hazardous to himself to return to the status of a private citizen, 'and might be dangerous to the public to have the government placed again under the control of the people', he resolved to maintain the status quo.

The tricky part was retaining autocratic power within the framework of the Republican system. On 13 January 27 BC, Octavian, having entered upon his seventh consulship, his fifth in succession, addressed the Senate, offering to lay down his extraordinary powers and surrender command of the armed forces. In his own words, 'after I had extinguished civil wars, having by universal consent been put in possession of supreme authority, I transferred the commonwealth from my own power to the control of the Senate and the Roman People.'

The Senate, naturally, refused to countenance such an act of self-abnegation. Feigning the reluctance appropriate to such an occasion, Octavian agreed to retain his consular and tribunician powers, and take special responsibility for particular provinces, namely Gaul, Spain, and Syria, governing them through legates while exercising his authority in Rome. Octavian was scrupulous in, technically, remaining only *princeps*, 'first citizen' of Rome; in his epitaph he continued to maintain that from this time forward 'I stood above all in influence, but of power I had no more than my colleagues in each several magistracy.' But while retaining the shell of republican propriety Octavian had ensured that 23 of the 26 legions on permanent station remained under his personal control.

Of the more than 20 epitaphs that survive for those veterans settled in one of Octavian's new colonies, Ateste (Este), at least six took on a new cognomen, Actiacus, to commemorate their part in the victory. One of these Actiaci, Marcus Billienus, headed the ceremonial procession of the XI Legion into its new home and went on to be a town councillor. (Courtesy Graham Sumner)

A new title had yet to be found that symbolized the unique status of the principate. The answer lay in a famous line from a poem by Ennius, telling of how Romulus, 'By august omen founded the city of Rome.' On 16 January the conscript fathers, on the motion of Plancus, decreed the title Augustus should be conferred upon Octavian, the second founder of Rome.

This process reached its apotheosis in 8 BC, when a *senatus consultum* decreed that, just as the month Quintilis had been renamed July, so the month Sextilis would thenceforth be known as August. A new generation in Rome was reconciled to the powers of the *princeps* being embodied in the individual, not the office itself. All that remained to complete the transition to the imperial system was popular submission to the transfer of these powers by dynastic inheritance. This was achieved in AD 14 with the succession of Tiberius, adopted son of Augustus. There was not a whisper of protest, for by this time no one could contemplate any viable alternative. After all, wrote Tacitus, 45 years after the battle of Actium, 'Who was there left who could have known the Republic?'

VISITING THE SITES TODAY

Flying into Aktion National Airport (PVK), on the tip of the southern promontory framing the entrance to the Gulf of Ambracia, one can immediately appreciate Antony's poor judgement in determining the location of his camp. It was literally underneath the runway, which to this day is low-lying and surrounded by stagnant and swampy ponds.

Just north of the airport, on the far side of the gulf, is the modern town of Preveza, easily accessible by the recently constructed tunnel linking the two promontories. If you would prefer to wait for the next ferry, arriving by sea takes you under the guns of an Ottoman-era fort, the Castle of Christ Pantokrator.

Farther north again is the site of Nicopolis, the city Octavian founded in the wake of his victory and populated by settling veterans and draining the surrounding municipalities of their townspeople. Octavian also revived the Actia, the games second in significance only to the Olympics, which were held every four years up to the mid-3rd century. Nicopolis remained an important provincial centre into the Byzantine era until its decline into ruin during the 10th to 11th centuries. The highlights of any visit to the site include the Roman era odeion and nymphaeum and Byzantine era basilicas and walls; the proasteion, the sacred grove that was the venue for the Actia; and the structure Octavian erected to serve as a memorial to the campaign of 31 BC.

This latter is of the most interest to the military historian. It is located on the site of Octavian's camp on the heights of Mikalitzi, overlooking the bay; in its heyday it would have been a constant presence looming over Nicopolis. It was composed of a stoa more than 40m wide embracing an expansive open space on three sides. A long row of rams harvested from Antony and Cleopatra's warships adorned the immense podium of the structure. A dedicatory inscription celebrated Octavian's victory 'in the name of the war waged on behalf of the Republic,' and consecrated the area, appropriately, to Neptune and Mars, the gods of the sea and of war. The memorial is little more than a pile of rubble today, but many of the sockets to which the rams were attached retain their original proportions, hinting at the power inherent in this ultimate manifestation of the naval weapons technology of the classical age.

BIBLIOGRAPHY

Of the surviving works of the ancient writers, Appian cuts off just as the conflict between Antony and Octavian heats up, leaving us with Dio and the second-rate accounts of Orosius, Florus, and Paterculus, plus the life of Antony in Plutarch, the life of Octavian in Suetonius, and whatever can be gleaned from the historians Josephus, Nicolaus, Strabo, and Pliny the Elder, and the poets Virgil, Horace and Lucan. Significant secondary sources, in addition to those cited in Campaign 199, *Philippi 42 BC*, include:

Casson, Lionel, and Steffy, J. Richard, *The Athlit Ram*, Texas A&M University Press, College Station, 1991.

Carter, John M., *The Battle of Actium*, Weybright & Talley, New York, 1970.

Foley, Vernard, and Soedel, Werner, 'Ancient Oared Warships', *Scientific American*, Vol. 244, No. 4, April 1981, pp. 148–63.

Gardiner, Robert (ed.), *The Age of the Galley*, Conway, London, 2004.

Gurval, Robert, *Actium and Augustus*, University of Michigan Press, Ann Arbor, 2001.

Harrington, Drew, 'The Battle of Actium – A Study in Historiography', *Ancient World*, Vol. IX, No. 1–2, May 1984, pp. 59–64.

Henderson, John Graham, *Fighting for Rome: Poets and Caesars, History and Civil War*, Cambridge University Press, Cambridge, 1998.

Kleiner, Diana E.E., *Cleopatra and Rome*, Harvard University Press, Cambridge, 2005.

Morrison, J.S., *Greek and Roman Oared Warships*, Oxbow Books, Oxford, 1996.

Murray, William M., 'Recovering Rams from the Battle of Actium: Experimental Archaeology at Nicopolis', in Konstantinos L. Zachos (ed.), *Proceedings of the Second International Nicopolis Symposium (11–15 September 2002)*, Actia Nicopolis Foundation, Preveza, 2007.

Murray, William M., 'Reconsidering the Battle of Actium – Again', in Vanessa B. Gorman and Eric W. Robinson (eds.), *Oikistes*, Brill, Boston, 2002, pp. 339–56.

Murray, William M., 'The Development and Design of Greek and Roman Warships (399 to 30 B.C.)', *Journal of Roman Archaeology*, Vol. 12, 1999, pp. 520–25.

Murray, William M., and Petsas, Photias M., 'Octavian's Campsite Memorial for the Actian War', *Transactions of the American Philosophical Society*, Vol. 79, Part 4., The American Philosophical Society, Philadelphia, 1989.

Ornstein, J. Orna, 'Ships on Roman Coins', *Oxford Journal of Archaeology*, Vol. 14, No. 2, July 1995, pp. 179–200.

Tarn, W.W., and Charlesworth, M.P., *Octavian, Antony and Cleopatra*, Cambridge University Press, Cambridge, 1965.

INDEX